The Horse Whisperer

The Horse Whisperer

When he talks, horses listen

Andrew Froggatt

with Leslie Van Gelder

ALLEN&UNWIN
SYDNEY·MELBOURNE·AUCKLAND·LONDON

In the chapter, 'The person within: Horses as friends', pages 191–205, the four girls' real names have not been used.

First published in 2016

Allen & Unwin
Level 3, 228 Queen Street
Auckland 1010, New Zealand

Phone: (64 9) 377 3800
Email: info@allenandunwin.com
Web: www.allenandunwin.co.nz

83 Alexander Street
Crows Nest NSW 2065, Australia
Phone: (61 2) 8425 0100

A catalogue record for this book is available
from the National Library of New Zealand

ISBN 978 1 877505 67 6

Internal design by Kate Frances Design
Set in 13/18 pt Baskerville by Midland Typesetters, Australia
Printed and bound in Australia by Griffin Press

10 9 8 7 6 5 4 3 2 1

MIX
Paper from
responsible sources
FSC® C009448
www.fsc.org

The paper in this book is FSC® certified.
FSC® promotes environmentally responsible,
socially beneficial and economically viable
management of the world's forests.

Contents

Introduction

It's early morning in the valley of Dalefield. Coronet Peak tops the tawny hills to the north, and the jagged grey peaks of the Remarkables frame the sky to the south. I call quietly to Chance, my twelve-year-old bay mare. She comes almost without my asking, happy to see me after a cold night under the stars. I pull off the rug which has been protecting her from the chill of the Wakatipu night. 'There's a good girl,' I tell her, using the same voice I use with my seven-month-old daughter, Tilly. Chance stands still while I rub her forehead. I know she loves the touch.

Bobby, our little black labrador puppy, is rolling around at Chance's feet, hoping to get some attention. But Chance barely has eyes for Bobby—she's looking at me. I am just beginning the process of taking her from being a brood mare, which she was for a long time, to being a demonstration horse. In the leadership courses I teach, the demonstration horses show my clients what they'll be able to do with their own horse. My horses always have a little something extra and help people to appreciate how amazing horses can be.

Many years ago Chance was brought to me as a talented horse who finished races in last place. With the right care and training, she became a race-winning horse, then as a brood mare she produced a beautiful son named Cool Guy. He's also destined to be a racehorse. For a while Chance might have forgotten she was a race-winner, but we're working on waking it up in her again.

Chance has spent the last five years more or less as a paddock mate, watching the other horses have their moment in the sun. Now she is coming into her own again. In the arena her long brown legs lift her up gracefully, and when I ask, she slows and comes to a complete stop just before my hand. Can she do this every time? No, not yet. Does she know me so well she can tell what I want from her by the way I hold my head? No, not yet. Will we get there? Absolutely. I've never had a horse who didn't.

When people ask me what I do I tell them I teach personal development and leadership through horses. When they ask me what I *can* do, though, the answer is a little different.

I can get something from a horse few other people can, as I seem to understand them in a way that is more like speaking their language than speaking ours. It's what is sometimes called horse whispering. I prefer to think of it as having a good dose of horse sense and taking the time to get to know the horse really well.

I'm not a fan of books in which the great horse whisperer tells you about all the famous people's horses in whose big ears he's whispered, but never tells you anything practical or useful. My hope with this book is that if you're someone who loves horses, from close up or afar, there'll be something in it of use to you. And even if you have never spent time with horses at all, but are interested in leadership or relationships, I hope this book will be just as useful. Although I began my career working with so-called problem horses, today a big part of what I do is about using horses to help people, and my partner Sam and I have a business we call Lead the Way. Whether it's business leaders, athletes or troubled young people, horses are a brilliant way to help people gain confidence and learn about themselves.

I still work with troubled or difficult horses, and there's no greater joy than in helping a horse to become happy and reach its potential. I've never met a horse who couldn't learn. I've never met a horse whose problems I couldn't fix, though some take more time than others. I truly believe the horses are grateful to me for helping them. The last thing they want is to spend their lives full of tension and worry, so if I can release a lot of their baggage they can move through life happier. I want to give them the confidence to handle life's surprises, so they can live peacefully, knowing that when they think and use their brains, they can handle any situation. It probably applies to people, too, though I confess I tend to have a lot more patience with horses than I do with people. Maybe by talking less, horses say more. They can certainly communicate, and I am always keen to listen to what they have to say.

With no words at all, horses can teach us about consistency, trust, communication and leadership. Above all, horses teach us about relationships. The only limitations are our willingness to learn, and time. I have been very lucky over the years to have had the privilege of learning from some amazing horses.

From wild horses to winners

LOCO AND MAVERICK

The first horses to arrive in New Zealand, a stallion and two mares, landed at Rangihoua in the Bay of Islands with the missionary Samuel Marsden, on 22 December 1814. Marsden was the great-great-great-uncle of my partner, Sam, so we feel a strong sense of connection to the man who introduced horses to this country. Amazingly, less than a hundred years later there were over 400,000 horses in New Zealand.

Today, it is estimated New Zealand's horse population is somewhere around 120,000, with 40,000 in the racing industry, the rest being recreational or work horses of some kind. Though there are few true wild horses, every horse who will eventually be ridden needs to be 'broken in', or 'started'. That's where people like me come in.

There are a few terms used around the subject of 'breaking in' that are worth talking about. The very phrase 'breaking in' has negative connotations for some people, because obviously something gets broken during the process—maybe the horse's spirit. Today some use the term 'taming' to refer to the first parts of the process, then 'touching' and 'handling' for the later stages. I tend to think about what I do as 'starting' a horse, though at times I use all the different terms interchangeably. To me it's all about starting a horse out right.

About ten years ago I had the privilege of starting twelve wild horses at Mt Nicholas Station, one of the twelve stations which ring Lake Wakatipu. It's a huge station, over 40,000 hectares, and the only road access is either via the neighbouring Walter Peak Station or through the back road that leads out to Mavora Lakes. Back in the day it was serviced by the old steamer TSS *Earnslaw*, but today Southern Discoveries' red and white catamarans carry visitors across the lake. It's a pretty spectacular spot.

Back then I was based about an hour up the coast from Wellington. We had a Canadian farrier who was also a hunting guide and regularly took people deerstalking around the back country near Queenstown. One day, when he was putting shoes on the horses for us, he asked me if I knew anyone who might want to come down to Queenstown, as he was doing a lot of hunting at Mt Nicholas Station, and they had some beautiful horses out in the mountains. The old guy who used to break in the station's horses for them had died, but they had continued to breed the horses and now they were everywhere.

I loved the idea of getting to work with wild horses on one of those big high-country stations, so I gave the station owner a call and set things up. A month later my partner and I went down there. The plan was we would go down for a month and break in twelve horses. We would then be given two of the horses to bring back with us so we could promote them in the North Island: once we'd helped establish his name he'd be able to sell more of his horses in the future.

Mt Nicholas is one of the most beautiful places I've ever been, and the idea of these wild horses who had been raised free in the Southern Alps was pretty damned appealing. The morning after we arrived that first time, the owner took off mustering for a week, so we were on our own to get the lie of the land. He'd set us up really well, letting us use his cattle yards, which were on the flats above the lakeshore. Before we arrived, he and his crew had put 30 horses into a big paddock so we could get a good look at them. Many of them were beautiful—big chestnuts and tall greys—and looking at them in that setting was just magical. We took our time observing them in the paddock, then we ran them into smaller yards where we picked out the twelve we were going to work with. As for the rest, we opened the gates and watched them gallop away, back up into the hills. If we hadn't been there to do the job of starting them, I could have stayed and just watched them run all day.

Breaking in horses is incredibly physical work. We'd start at 6.30 with a good hearty breakfast at the cookhouse, then we'd work through until 9.30 in the evening. The cook treated us well, though, and there were almost always hot scones and good coffee for morning tea, and a thermos and cake in the afternoons.

No one ever taught me how to catch a wild horse. Some horses can be quick to catch, while for others it's a time thing, whereby they need to trust us more to let us in closer. Lots of patience and understanding are needed to erase their fears. Wild horses can be very different from domestic ones. These horses had had very little contact with humans—maybe being branded when they were six months old, but otherwise they really hadn't been touched—so just the thought of us was overwhelming to them. In many ways, during that first week they were more like terrified sheep than horses. I would walk into the cattle yards and off they'd go, flying up to the other end as one big thundering herd. These were metal yards and often in their desperation to get away from me the horses would smash into the rails or rattle them. We had to move quietly around them and be very conscious of our energy levels, which I'll explain more about below.

If they hadn't been so frightened it would have been almost comical. Here I was weighing 80 kilograms and they could easily weigh 600 kilograms, but they were looking across at me as if I was the one who could crush them, instead of the other way round. These were four-, five- and six-year-old horses, so they were already big, strong, mentally tough—despite their fear—and very set in their ways.

Our plan was pretty simple. Over the span of four weeks we wanted to take them from being these frightened creatures to horses we could handle easily, who could trot and canter with riders on their backs. No bucking. No rearing. Just plain, good solid horses. Needless to say, we had our work cut out for us, especially in that first week when the horses wouldn't let us touch them. Our first main objective was to get a head collar on each horse. While it sounds relatively easy, it wouldn't happen until we had reached the stage of being able to touch the horse, and for it to be desensitised enough to allow us to put the collar on.

No one ever taught me how to catch a wild horse.

In many ways wild horses are the opposite of domesticated horses, which can often be pushy at the beginning of a working relationship because they are so used to humans. Wild horses are very respectful and they keep their distance, largely because of their fear. The beauty of working with them is that they haven't developed any bad habits, so we don't have to go about undoing those. Instead we can start them out the right way from the beginning.

With horses like these, my very first goal is to get them to face me. My method is quite tedious, perhaps, in comparison with the old way, where horses were lassoed and then left to thrash for a long time as a way of breaking their spirit. Instead, I work with them so they learn basic respect. In the first day I am constantly trying to turn them because they want to turn away from me and show me their backsides. Horses are great avoiders, and wild horses are the Olympic champions of this. So the first goal is to be able to say 'Look at me' and to have them turn and face me. It's basic respect—and it's also dangerous to meet their back end.

ONE OF THE BENEFITS of working with wild horses is they provide a great way to learn about our own energy levels around horses, as they are super-sensitive. One of the horses, whom we named Loco, from the Spanish word for 'crazy', demonstrated this perfectly.

A chestnut mare with a big star and a white sock, Loco moved more like a stag than a horse, snorting and tossing her head, taking huge floating strides as she moved across the ground. Even before I entered her yard, Loco was snorting and carrying on. I came in ever so quietly, but even though she and I were alone in the pen, with plenty of space between us, I could see she was terrified. I watched her quietly, and though she was pawing the ground and snorting, there was nothing but naked fear in her eyes. I quietly lit a cigarette and stood still while I smoked it. I was 4 metres away from her and I just wanted to give her some time with me that close before I ventured any nearer. When I was done with my cigarette I took one very small, low-energy step towards her, and in that instant she jumped and cleared the top rail of the cattle yard. I was amazed at how just taking one small step in her direction had sent her leaping over the yards. But I also couldn't help but think, 'What a jumper! I'll be taking you home.'

A chestnut mare with a big star and a white sock, Loco moved more like a stag than a horse, snorting and tossing her head, taking huge floating strides as she moved across the ground.

My energy matters. Even though I was as quiet and calm as I could be, Loco still felt my presence as if I was right on top of her and she had nowhere to go. So when I am first working with wild horses, it's important I back away and take the pressure off as soon as they turn and face me. It's the instant timing of the release that lets the horse know it's done the right thing.

I keep taking a step towards the horse until I can be in its space. At the beginning, I might be a metre or two away from the horse and it will react as if I were standing right on top of it, creating too much pressure. It's all about pressure, and with wild horses, just my presence alone creates pressure. My presence at 2 metres is pressure. Probably just the thought of me is pressure.

So we have to go really slowly. With domesticated horses, my praise, touch, and the release from pressure all combine to be a positive for the horse. With wild horses, touch is a long way off, but they still hear the tone of my voice, and most of all they respond to the release of pressure. In that first stage, all I'm asking of them is to turn and face me. I want to get them to the stage where I can move around the yard on the rails, with the horse in the middle, and it will be turning and facing me all the time.

Once they are doing that, I will take a step towards them. Just one step, but they might start to back away as if to say, 'Hey, I'm just not comfortable with you getting that close to me.' So we begin a dance of 'advance and retreat' for a while as I stop and step back, taking the pressure off them. And then, when they seem ready again and can bear it, I'll take another step in. All along the way, I expect them to keep looking at me and not to turn away.

I'll be honest, it's tedious. Step. Wait. Absorb the feeling. Back away. Step. Wait. Back away. Respond. Step. Wait. Over and over again. Eventually, maybe after a few hours, I can reach out and touch the horse's nose. While for me it's just reaching out and touching a nose, for the horse it's all new and its adrenaline will be pumping. Some will pin their ears back in the hope of intimidating me, so I step away. It doesn't really work on me, but I always give them credit for wanting to give it a try. What they don't know is that I tend to have tired arms at the end of that day, as I've been reaching out and up a lot as I work to come closer and closer and then take the pressure away—over and over again. Many times when I reach out, they'll turn their heads, try to look away, and then we begin again. Increasingly, though, inch by inch,

I get closer and closer until there is nowhere to go but to look at me and to let me touch them on the nose. The only way to get them to that stage is to spend the time with them. The more intensely I work, the more they have to try.

With those first few touches, I have to be ready for just about anything because the first time they make physical contact with me it can scare the life out of them. I love this part as it's an intensely special moment where we are together in that space, and our relationship builds from there. It's a real connection of trust. But anything could still happen, so I have to be calm and centred in myself. I need to convey to the horse that everything is perfectly fine and there's nothing to worry about. They're learning how to be in this relationship from me, and they're taking their cue about drama or worry or all the things to do with this relationship from how I meet them. It helps that I know more or less the range of reactions I'm likely to see from them. While this kind of touch is new to them and incredibly scary, I've been there before so I can see them through. I always say that around wild horses you need to be 'relaxed but ready', as both states are extremely important.

It's also interesting working out where each individual will let me touch it. For some it might be the nose. For others it's the cheek—they might turn their heads and let me touch them there but nowhere else. Wherever it is, that becomes my first go-to point. Then I move bit by bit around their heads until I get them to the stage where I can come in on one side and touch them on the neck. Then I can begin to think about getting the head collar on. It's a long process to get to this point, but it's worth taking the time because at each stage I'm taking away that high level of sensitivity and replacing it with familiarity.

I need to convey to the horse that everything is perfectly fine and there's nothing to worry about.

The horses have to experience a lot of new sensations when they're working with humans. While we might take for granted how a rope might feel, to the horse this can be another frightening experience. With the horses at Mt Nicholas, once they were letting me touch their heads I would rub them on the neck with baling twine so they got used to the feeling of something other than my hand against their bodies. They had to be desensitised to each new thing they were going to experience otherwise, when they encountered it at some later time, they might blow it out of proportion and panic.

With some of the horses, touching them on the face still proved to be too much. In those cases, because we were working with some time pressure, I'd get the lead rope on them and would touch that instead, as if it were an extension of my arm. I'd run my hand up the rope, getting closer to them until I could touch them. In a way they were a bit like some kids, when just saying you're going to tickle them has them giggling, but taking a step towards them is almost too much. For some of the wild horses it was just like this, and their varying sensitivities were both fascinating and challenging.

Once we got the head collars on and the lead ropes clipped, then we could begin basic groundwork. We moved to touching the horses with ropes, around their legs and everywhere else, so they could get used to the idea of being touched all over their bodies. The ropes became safe extensions of our own arms. From there, we worked on getting them to lead well so that, when they felt the pressure of the lead rope, it encouraged them to move forward.

By the end of the first week the horses were doing really well. The cattle yards had been a good place to start but the ground was too stony for them, and a few were getting tender feet. Now I wanted to move them into yards half a kilometre away. We were only a few days into having the horses comfortable with the leads, and we had to move them down past the beach. Now we had to test ourselves to see if what we had been putting in place was going to work. One by one we led the horses by rope leads, and we were relieved when they responded well.

I had asked the station owner to put out some lucerne for the horses, so when they arrived in the new yards they were met with these big, beautiful bales. Once there, we established boundaries, taught the horses to back up and come forward, and also got them to lunge, which involves encouraging the horse to move in a circle around you. Lunging has a lot to do with learning how to respond to pressure and position. Initially, the horses don't always comprehend what's wanted, but after a little while they start to be able to move around you in a circle and you begin to establish the kind of conversation you want to be having.

These initial steps in groundwork are the same ones I take with all the horses I work with, and the goals are always exactly the same. I'm looking to build a relationship, teach the horse some basic manners, and ensure it is safe for me, or others, to work with. Over and over it all comes down to repetition and the ever-present thought I pass on to the horse: 'Show me again you can do what I've just asked.' What I want to see is what a good coach wants to see in his or her athletes—that with enough practice they can do it, and do it better and faster every time.

There was another component to training wild horses and this came a week and a half into the starting process. My partner jokingly called herself 'Queen of the Bag', and once wrote this was 'the most boring and tedious job known to man', which says something about how much fun it is. The idea is simple. A plastic bag is attached to the end of a long whip and the horse is touched all over its body with the bag. Then, when they're comfortable with the feel of the bag, it's shaken, too, so it's not just feel but sound and movement as well. I've spent whole days of my life shaking plastic bags around horses—who wouldn't want my job?— because it has a purpose and that purpose is a good one. We are literally shaking the fear out of the horses. Fear of the sound of a jacket flapping in the wind. Fear of something above its back or head. Fear of a bag that might fly up from the street.

What I'm working towards in bagging the horse is the point when it eventually drops its head and is relaxed at the sound or feel of the bag. Like many of the things I do with the horses, this just gets them to cross over from a place of innate worry to one of, 'Oh, that's OK, nothing too scary there,' which helps them live more successfully in our world. It teaches them to face their fears, so when they are confronted with an unexpected situation they think, as opposed to running first and thinking later.

When the Queen of the Bag got tired, I would sometimes ask other people to help out. They would wave the bag for maybe ten minutes then say, 'Yep, that horse is fine.' But I would see where the horse's head was and say, 'No, go back and do it some more. Do it until the horse is so used to the bag it hardly notices you.' At times bagging taught me as much about other people's levels of patience and thoroughness as it did about each horse's pent-up fears. I can't stress enough the necessity for thoroughness when working with horses, which means being patient and moving forward only when the horse is ready, not when we get bored.

Once we'd used bagging to get the fear out of the horses' upper bodies, we needed to do something similar with their legs. As my partner discovered when Maverick, one of the stronger horses, double-barrelled her early on (it's a nice expression for kicking with both legs at the same time—you can imagine the bruises), wild horses can easily use their legs as weapons. I want to make sure it's safe to walk around and behind a horse without the risk of that happening.

I also want to be able to safely pick up its feet or touch it anywhere I want.

While we did the lunge work with the horses we used a system of leg ropes to desensitise their legs. I don't find this part as difficult as some people do, perhaps because by this stage I've already been doing some lunge work, so the horse has grown to trust me. Adding another dimension by using the rope to encourage the horse to lift its foot just builds on what we've done before. I have them on a long lunge line and then, one foot at a time, I put another rope with a ring on it around each foot and feed the rope back on itself. Then I send the horse out on the lunge. Some horses think, 'What's that on my foot?' and run around madly. Others kick and kick. That's what we want them to do, so they can get it out of their system, and in the future, we, or the farrier, will never have to worry about handling the horse's feet.

So I send the horse out on the circle and have it walk around me. Then I take hold of the leg rope and ask it to stop and give to pressure. I'll talk about giving to pressure in more detail when I talk about groundwork later on. It's all about teaching horses not to get too worried if their leg is stuck in a fence, or if they're in a situation where someone has to hold their leg or foot.

I do the same at the trot, then I stand in front of the horse and ask it to give to pressure and lead from the leg, before starting to cue the horse to pick up its foot from the pressure of the rope. It's a really good, kind way of handling the legs and feet, rather than the old approach of hobbling or tying up the legs.

I often tell people who work with me that horses can be 'time bombs' unless we make sure they've been tested. I want to make sure that any tension in them has been released, as I don't want a horse who appears all relaxed with me to become difficult in someone else's hands. So we expose the horse to all kinds of situations to see how it will react. After I know I've got rid of a lot of the tension through the bagging and long-rope work with their feet, I move on to flank-roping. As well as releasing the tension and anxiety, I want them to learn that bucking is a big waste of energy and will only make them more and more tired. If they want to buck, they can get it out of their system now, but never with someone on their back.

Initially, I want the horse to become familiar with the feel of a rope around its belly. For a wild horse in particular, it's a new experience. Again, I use the flank-rope to help the horse gain confidence, and to teach it that something tightening across its middle isn't a reason to be fearful.

When we were doing this at Mt Nicholas, we tended to have an audience. While hours of getting a horse to stop in front of my hand isn't too exciting to watch, and bagging is no thrill, seeing a wild horse bucking for all its worth is something else. And I think the station's owner and the workers quite enjoyed coming round and sitting on the edge of the fence just to up the ante for me a little.

What I do is put a rope around the horse's body and feed it through a ring so I can do a quick release if necessary, then I move it into the girth position and send the horse out on the lunge. As the horse gets used to this I slip the rope back to the flanks. Horses respond to this in many different ways. Some will tear around at 100 miles an hour and try to outrun the rope—these are the ones who are likely to take off under saddle. Some turn into bucking broncos, and others, amazingly, just do nothing.

We work the horse one side and then the other until it stops. People are often surprised that it can be the quiet horses who have the most bucking in them. Then again, maybe it's like people—sometimes it's the quiet ones who turn out to have a whole lot tied up inside them. The best part of the exercise is when the horse realises that bucking is just plain hard work and it doesn't seem like so much fun anymore. The idea behind this exercise is to release all the tension, worry and fear from inside the horse so we don't have to ride it.

The best part of the exercise is when the horse realises that bucking is just plain hard work and it doesn't seem like so much fun anymore.

With this accomplished, the Mt Nicholas horses were ready to move on to the next stage, which is one everyone waits for—when I can begin to get up on their backs and get them ready for saddling and riding. After about two and a half or three weeks we were starting to lie on the horses bareback. Horses don't really want anyone up on their backs, but after a while they come to accept it as the way things are going to be. Everything comes down to repetition.

To begin to get them comfortable with this, I jump up on one side, and then come down to the ground again, over and over. After a while I'm able to jump up and lie across the middle of the horse's back. Then we start to work in pairs. I usually stand in front of the horse reading its body language and mood, while my partner continues to come up on its back until she can lie on the horse with her feet at its tail and her head resting on its mane. It's a beautiful sight to see someone being able to lie peacefully on the back of a horse which only a few weeks before wouldn't let anyone touch it.

Once the horse is used to the rider's weight, I slowly ease them up until they are facing in the right direction and they sit up on the horse for the first time. You can imagine how thrilled we were every time we were able to get there with these wild horses. In a way, being the first person to get up on the back of any horse is like landing on the moon and taking the first step—going someplace no one has ever been before!

The last stage of taming the wild horses is getting the saddle onto them. In the old days the guys who broke in horses used the same saddle for every horse no matter what its size. The result of this, however, was that many of the horses would have had a bad experience right from the start, which would have influenced how they felt through-out their riding lives.

I try to make sure each horse has a good experience. As I saddle up the horses one at a time, and then set them loose in the round yard, I'm looking to see if they are going to buck once they are having a good canter with the saddle on. Some horses might not be too bothered at the walk or trot, but the canter can be the pace where they react. Out of these twelve wild horses only one bucked, and it was only because of a slightly loose girth, which we were able to fix. Not too bad.

In a way, being the first person to get up on the back of any horse is like landing on the moon and taking the first step—going someplace no one has ever been before!

Having the saddle on the horse didn't mean we could suddenly ride off into the hills, no matter how appealing the surrounding mountains looked to us. First we had to get the horses used to the stirrups. We clanged and banged them so the horses got used to the sound, then we touched the horses with the stirrups so they'd feel them in all the different ways they might in their day-to-day riding life. It's similar to the bagging, as the idea is to get the horses used to whatever might come their way in everyday life. Saddles are shaken, and the horses are lunged on the long rope while walking, trotting and cantering. I want to know they are bombproof, and when I feel they are, then whoever is riding them can start to put some weight into the stirrups and riding movement in the saddle. And just when we think we've got it right, we do it again. And again.

We worked in pairs again during this phase, with the person in the saddle serving as a kind of test pilot. I'm always watching the horses' heads—if their heads shoot up I know they're not relaxed, but if they are, then I move on to steering and stopping. The first couple of steps are bloody hard work. They generally don't want to move forward, and they can just stand there for a long time pretending they don't understand what's being asked of them. But in time I get them to walk and then trot, and ultimately to canter.

My friend Catarina Strom was living in Queenstown at this time, and I took advantage of this to have another pair of expert hands. Catarina was the national coach of the New Zealand Vaulting Club, and she can do the most extraordinary gymnastics on the back of a horse. We had worked together up north quite a bit, so it was great to get her out for a few days with the horses just at the point when they were ready to be ridden. While she could have done backflips, no doubt, we were just glad all twelve of the horses could be ridden, and ridden well.

During this time, also, Jeremy Moon, the founder of Icebreaker, came down to the station with some of his team. Jeremy was a family friend of the station owners and had spent a lot of time at Mt Nicholas as a boy. The owners suggested I do a little workshop with the wild horses for the Icebreaker people. Even though the horses hadn't yet been ridden, we were able to do a leadership workshop where the Icebreaker people worked in pairs with the horses to get them to do some basic ground-work. It was amazing to have progressed from horses who just two weeks earlier had almost never been touched to horses who could be led and moved through their paces by corporate executives. I was a little nervous about how it would go, but it was a real boost to see the horses and the Icebreaker people working so well together. Although I had been doing pretty regular leadership courses for about three years at this point, this was the first time I had used horses who were this wild.

Finally, after four weeks, it was time for our last task—to get all twelve of the horses to comfortably learn how to go into the horse floats. While only two of them, Loco and Maverick, came home with us, we could have taken any one of those horses, and we would have been glad to have them.

Two years later I went back with an Australian woman who worked for us, and over two weeks we handled another fourteen wild horses, then took the top six back to Wellington to sell. Though there were a few problems— one of the horses broke its leg later on, and another went lame—on the whole the project worked really well. One of these horses, a grey called Brave, has been winning most of his show-hunter jumping classes, and another, Busito, is currently in the New Zealand under-20 dressage squad.

Wild horses are truly special because they have an innate toughness, and I love that about them. They can also teach us more about energy and sensitivity than any other type of horse. Plus, knowing they've never worked with humans before means I can start them out right and give them the best possible beginning. I love that.

Becoming a horse whisperer

KIWI, BOBBY AND COMET

If you believe most of the books about horse whisperers, I should have been born on the back of a horse and have learned to ride before I could walk or speak. Or perhaps I could have been raised in a stall with the horses, or been the next reincarnation of Phar Lap or Kiwi. I know it won't come as a surprise I wasn't born in a manger. All in all, my beginnings in the world were pretty uneventful.

There's always the riddle of why one child becomes horse-mad while another, with exactly the same upbringing, takes no interest in horses. In my case, the mystery to my patient parents was not that I was horse-mad—it was that I stayed that way.

I blame it on two things. The first of these was the fact that my grandfather had a farm in the Ohariu Valley near Wellington where his racehorses came home to rest. The second was Kiwi, the horse who won the Melbourne Cup in 1983.

My birthday is 1 August, the same day as all the horses in New Zealand and Australia, since, because of the way records are kept, all horses share a common birthday. Though I'd like to think otherwise, I'm fairly sure this is a coincidence, but it's a good one. I can say, though, my affinity for horses began in earnest on 1 November 1983, three months after my tenth birthday.

I had just come home from another unmemorable day at school. Those spring days were dragging on, as they do when you're ten. Like kids all over New Zealand, I just wanted school to be over so I could go out and spend time on the farm. But that Tuesday was different, because it was Melbourne Cup day. While I didn't know it yet, I was about to see something that would be a big game-changer for me.

In the spring of 1983 I didn't own a horse. My mother loved birds, but maybe because she had been raised on the farm, she wasn't so keen on horses. And though my younger brother Nick and I begged for a dog, Dad thought a dog needed more land than we had, so we only had one animal, a pretty tough farm cat. My grandparents' farm, on the other hand, had dogs, horses, sheep and cattle. It was just

6 kilometres from where we lived. As a ten-year-old boy there was no place on earth I wanted to be more than on that farm.

I think that as soon as I could walk, or climb up on a fence, I was rubbing and petting the horses on my grandfather's farm. I loved the farm, all of it, but the highlight was the horses. Grandfather had always farmed, and so had his father. Mum's brother, Greg, worked on the farm with Grandfather, so I idolised those two. I loved helping out around the place, going on the truck and feeding the farm dogs, or mixing up the horses' feed and feeding them. And I was always pestering my grandfather about getting a horse of my own.

I used to read my grandfather's racing magazines, too, like *Bloodhorse*, flipping through them, looking at the pictures. We had a chair with a lift-up seat where magazines were hidden. I loved that chair, and would spend hours with my head down, turning the dog-eared pages of those magazines just looking at horses. It must have been in one of those magazines I first read about Kiwi.

My parents used to put the TV news on every night, so the night before the Melbourne Cup we were all watching when they showed the top horses getting tucked up in bed in their stables. Then the picture moved from the stables to a clip of Kiwi, just grazing somewhere an hour outside of Melbourne in a big paddock with a mob of sheep. He looked so damned happy. I loved it.

The next day I rushed home from school and sat down on the couch to watch the Melbourne Cup. For most of the race, Kiwi just sort of plodded along in the back field. The race caller didn't mention him until the last 600 metres, when he suddenly moved down the straight. Even now, 32 years later, when I watch a video of that race I can feel my heart in my throat as Kiwi just goes for it—seeing him come from behind and pass horse after horse along the outside of the track; hearing the race caller's voice change as if even he can't believe what he's seeing. It was a kind of miracle, as Kiwi surprised everyone who had underestimated him to come from dead last to win the Melbourne Cup.

But Kiwi didn't become my inspiration because he won the race. It was because he had been allowed to be what he was—a farm horse—and when he was encouraged to give his best, he did. He gave even more than that, and went from being a $1000 horse Snowy Lupton, a wiry old farmer from Waverley, had bought for his wife to trot around the farm to one of the greatest racehorses in New Zealand history.

No one should ever have underestimated Kiwi, the horse who spent the night before the Cup out in the paddock. He didn't just win the race. What struck a really deep chord in me was he seemed to be a much happier horse than any of the others. It's amazing how much power basic happiness can give a creature—whether it's a horse or a person. For me, it started there—the idea that to get the very best out of a horse it had to be happy. It's common sense really. Kiwi had been trained and stimulated on the farm, working and doing what was asked of him. His owners saw his talent and encouraged it. Through their understanding they had brought out the best in Kiwi, and in turn Kiwi won the biggest staying race in the world for them.

That idea became the foundation for everything I've wanted to do ever since that day. Although it hasn't happened yet, and I think it's fair to say I've got some work to do, among my goals is to develop a relationship with a horse I could take to the Melbourne Cup, and win. I still want to do it the same way as Snowy Lupton did with Kiwi: training a horse on the farm, keeping him outside, and creating an environment where he would thrive.

It's amazing how much power basic happiness can give a creature—whether it's a horse or a person. For me, it started there—the idea that to get the very best out of a horse it had to be happy.

I've spent the last 25 years learning how to bring out the best in every horse I meet. But winning the Melbourne Cup with a horse like Kiwi? Well, wouldn't that be something?

WHEN I WAS YOUNG I read all the books about horse whisperers that had started coming out, mostly from the States, hoping to find some good tips. Instead, I got the sense they were more about power in relationships than anything else. A lot of the American books seemed to be more about heavy-handed fathers than about horses. They talked about guys who had come to their understanding of horses because they had witnessed or experienced cruelty to horses and to children, and they had tried to do something about it by developing a really strong understanding of their relationships with horses.

Much of what is known as natural horsemanship, which is based on the idea of a more humane approach to working with horses, has evolved to try to address these issues of power. I get it. I think for me, though, it's more about a deeper understanding of what fosters a horse's happiness, a horse like Kiwi. I'm of a different generation to a lot of those guys. Most of them grew up around horses as a way of life, so they would have taken on board some of the old practices which I think can be the opposite of what they hope to achieve in the long term.

A while ago, when I went to a workshop given by one of the big high-flyers in the field, I had an experience that really brought this home. I had been looking forward to this workshop, because I was sure I was going to take away a huge collection of new tools and ideas I could use with the horses. Instead I took away a big lesson in what *not* to do.

In this case, someone who'd attended one of this guy's courses before had come up with a solution for a bucking horse. He ran fishing twine through its mouth, up to the top of the bridle, then took it back and tied it to the top of the saddle. So whenever the horse tried to put its head down to buck, it couldn't get it down because the fishing twine started cutting into its mouth. Eventually, to stop the pain, the horse stopped putting its head down. I hate the idea of creating pain-related quick fixes for behavioural problems, and I was also surprised no one thought to look into whether or not the horse was bucking because of back problems. But this was someone else's course, and I was there to learn. The guy running the workshop had been passing on this idea for a while, and plenty of people had picked it up as a solution for their bucking horses.

During the talk, someone in the audience said he wanted to thank this fellow because he'd learned this technique at a workshop a year or two earlier and he'd found it hugely successful when he'd tried it with his horse. The trainer said he was pleased to hear that, until the man said he'd been riding his horse that way ever since. The technique had only been intended to be used two or three times until the horse understood, and this poor horse had had fishing twine in its mouth for the last two years!

It's stories like these that break my heart and make me really angry. Even if the trainer didn't intend the man to keep doing this to his horse, he had introduced it as a solution, the man had taken it on board, and because he didn't know any better, he hadn't known when to stop. I would rather have no training than that kind.

I am largely self-taught, which means things may have been missed from my education. What I don't have, though, is baggage I'm going to have to unload at some point. I'm not perpetuating teachings from traditions that no longer have a place in the way we interact with horses. Instead, I've had a string of really excellent teachers, all of whom have had four legs, and I've also taken bits from various trainers and incorporated them into my own system.

The first of those four-legged teachers was an old pony named Bobby.

I've had a string of really excellent teachers, all of whom have had four legs, and I've also taken bits from various trainers and incorporated them into my own system.

I was ten when my grandfather finally gave in and presented my brother Nick and me with a little Paint pony named Bobby, with a chestnut-spotted white face. He had been grazing on the farm and was owned by a guy who did a lot of breaking in around the district. So the year 1983 was a real turning point for me—it wasn't just the year Kiwi won the Melbourne Cup, it was also the year I got my first horse.

At first Nick and I used to argue about who was going to spend time with Bobby. Who's going to go to the farm today? Who's going to brush him? Who's going to ride him? Truth is, caring for a horse never really works in pairs. But my brother wasn't as keen on Bobby as I was—actually, I'm not sure anyone could have been as keen as I was. I probably always had a sensitive side, which I still consider to be one of my strengths with horses, as it enables me to see things from their point of view. But back then, I just spent a hell of a lot of time with Bobby.

About the same time, one of the people who would become one of my best friends for life moved into our street. Rich was also keen on horses. Together we would walk the 6 kilometres over to Grandfather's farm on the weekend, and we'd spend all day hanging out over there.

I really knew nothing about looking after a horse apart from having a really quiet, patient way with him, and a huge desire to always make him happy and ensure he was OK. Bobby was a tough old thing, and he had a lot to teach me. He was about twenty when I got him, and he had a long history of young kids wanting to learn to ride him, so he could become wily when he didn't want to be ridden.

He had a good little trick. When we'd try to catch him, he'd pin his ears back with a nasty expression and then rear up and strike at us. Rich and I would sprint away and Bobby would chase us. Sometimes we'd just sprint and jump the fence, then spend the next two hours calling him. Eventually one of us would sheepishly go and find my uncle Greg and ask him if he'd catch Bobby for us.

It took a while, but eventually we learned from Greg that what we had to do was stand our ground. Bobby was all talk. He'd rear up and rear up, but apart from being noisy and a little scary he wouldn't actually follow through. So if we just stood there and let him get it all out of his system, then we could catch him.

I always felt sorry for Bobby because he wasn't an important horse to anyone except a ten-year-old boy. He didn't have rugs or covers or get fed. Grandfather was busy running the farm, so he didn't really have time to tell me what to do or how to look after him. The guy who had owned him showed us a few more things, but I didn't like the way he was with the horses.

I don't know how it is that, even as a young kid, you know the way someone is doing something is wrong. Maybe it was just how it felt to me. I've spent most of my life trusting my instincts when it comes to horses, and I guess a lot of my knowledge has developed out of seeing other people do silly things around them. It's mostly just common sense, but I've learned even that is sometimes in short supply.

There used to be a local horse-breaker who grazed horses on my grandfather's farm, and sometimes I would watch him. He would do things like tie their heads to their tails, then he'd get in his car and drive off, leaving the horses like that for several hours. Then he'd come back and tie their heads on the other side, so they'd just walk slowly round and round the paddock like that. Imagine how sore their muscles must have been after a whole day. I know now that it was just the traditional way of breaking in a horse, but it seemed wrong to me even then. Sometimes when he drove off I'd sneak over and say, 'Oh, this has come off . . .' And other times, when he had freed them, Rich and I would go over and rub them and pet them.

It's not surprising every horse he had there used to hate him and run away from him. You can break a horse and turn it into an animal who fears you, but is that horse ever going to give you its best?

In his own way, Bobby was quite patient with me, and now as I look back I can see Grandfather was, too. I wanted Bobby to have a bridle so I took one of my grandfather's racehorse bridles, which was massive on this poor little pony, and then I put it on him without a saddle. Sometimes I would just clamber on and ride around the farm bareback, then I'd fall off him. If I saw something in the shed like one of my grandfather's big covers, I'd put it on him. I used to take him feed from the shed, and give him treats. I thought he should have everything the racehorses had.

You can break a horse and turn it into an animal who fears you, but is that horse ever going to give you its best?

The idea that has served me throughout my whole life in working with horses is a really simple one I learned with Bobby. Be nice and kind and build a relationship. Everything is about putting in the time with the horse—that's how real relationships are built. But if you're spending a lot of time with your horses, looking after them, building up the relationship, you should be getting results. If you're not getting results, you're doing something wrong. It's not just time, but the quality of the time together that matters.

People often tell me they've been riding horses for twenty years, but it might be an hour's riding lesson once a week for twenty years, which is just four hours a month. It's not the same as someone who's spending fourteen hours a week with their horse, and it will be reflected in the results they get.

Bobby was my best friend. We used to chat away all the time. I think it's similar for many kids and their horses, and plenty of adults as well. You can tell horses things you can't always tell other people. They listen really well. Or at least Bobby did.

But as I grew from a ten-year-old boy into a thirteen-year-old, with a twenty-year-old pony who was starting to show its age, I started to look for another horse to keep up with my teenage energy. The guy who had owned Bobby had another pony who had already been broken in, and now he wanted to sell it. Comet was a black pony with a star on his forehead. He was a bit of a handful, and I was always a little bit scared of him, but I said I'd really like to look after Bobby and Comet at the same time.

Comet was beautiful, but he was an arrogant little fellow. Even way back then, that was what I looked for in my own horses. I love the X factor—a 'Look at me, I'm the best' sort of attitude—but the key is getting it working with or for you rather than against you.

Going from Bobby, who was really quiet and mostly good-natured, to Comet, who was a horse with a lot of energy and spark in him, meant at first I was a bit out of my depth. But as with Bobby, I just spent lots and lots of time with him. Eventually I got Comet to do anything I wanted. He just loved to jump. I'd set up jumps and measure how high the fences were and then set up jumps we could do together. I'd jump bareback with him, and we'd spend hours and hours playing around.

Comet was the first horse I ever sold. I told my grandfather, and anyone else who'd listen to me, I was going to sell him for a thousand dollars. They all said, 'You won't get a thousand dollars for him,' but I stuck to my guns and it's exactly what I did get. He was worth every cent, too.

Bobby was still my best mate, though. As we both got older, I spent more time just taking care of Bobby, while Comet got more of the work. I knew vaguely that Bobby couldn't live forever, but when you're a kid you don't think about how long a horse's life is going to be, because it's already been longer than your own has been. I never imagined he wouldn't be there.

I was in my first year at Wellington College when Bobby started to go downhill. One day, Greg rang early in the morning to say that Bobby had colic. Colic can be deadly for horses. They get a twist in the gut and it's really uncomfortable. Horses can't vomit, so instead they roll around. My uncle had found Bobby rolling around under the macrocarpa trees at the edge of his house.

They had already had the vet out by the time I got there at about nine. Bobby was alive, but he was out in the paddock heavily doped on medication. I sat there on an old bucket taking in the thought I had almost lost him, and I stayed there until about five that evening watching over him. I can still remember sitting on the bucket all day, just rubbing Bobby and talking to him. It was my first real brush with death.

Bobby survived that time, but a few years later the inevitable happened. In a life that seems to have followed long circles laid out along a line of Melbourne Cup days and national horse birthdays, it was six years after I had watched Kiwi cross the finish line that Bobby crossed a different one.

I had come home from college excited at the thought of watching another Melbourne Cup. But Mum didn't look quite right. She sat down on the couch with me and said, 'Andrew, Bobby's had an accident, a fall down the gully.' And that was it. I never saw him again. I cried for days and threw myself into working Comet. On that day I also promised myself that every horse who came my way would always have the best, and I would become the best as well, so I would be able to achieve that.

I made a commitment then that I was going to work with horses. And I knew I was going to have to go further than the farm to learn what I needed to know.

Learning to listen

BEANIE

When I first met Beanie, he just about never had all four feet on the ground at the same time. A bay with a white blaze across his face and three white socks, Beanie's speciality was rearing up. He also did his best to intimidate people whenever he didn't get his own way. By the time I met him, he had been left in a paddock with almost nothing done with him for a year. With his feet up in the air, he let everyone know he wasn't too happy.

Beanie struggled most around the float. Every time he was brought into it, he flew backwards, desperate to get out, and then reared and reared, trying to get away. This, in particular, was what had given Beanie his reputation for being a horse who rarely had all four feet on the ground.

Working with horses like Beanie forms a large part of what I do. Much of this has to do with learning how to read the horse and understanding what's happening in its mind and body—the aim is to figure out how much is attitude, and how much is possibly the result of pain. If horses could talk, this would all be a lot easier, but in a way they are talking to us all the time; it's just a question of learning how to listen to what they are saying.

A horse's greatest power is its ability to reflect back to us who we are, in effect acting as an emotional mirror. They reflect and respond to our energy, to our relationship with time, and to our ability to walk the talk. How do we interpret that, though? Sometimes the best way is simply to look more closely at the horse. To clear up a couple of myths and make it easier to understand them, I want to talk a little about horses' bodies and their history.

A horse's greatest power is its ability to reflect back to us who we are, in effect acting as an emotional mirror.

Horses have been around for a very long time—56 million years, in one form or another. They started out as small creatures, *Eohippus*, which were about the size of a poodle. They had three toes on each foot, which helped them make their way through what was largely a hot and swampy world at that time. They didn't have the long, graceful gait they have today, but probably scampered along in their wet world like little dogs.

While horses have changed a lot in shape and size over time, what has not changed is that they have always been prey animals. Horses were never out hunting down other creatures, or at least not until humans starting riding on their backs, and even then they didn't have a hunting instinct. They have always been the hunted ones.

Being prey animals over millions of years has made horses simultaneously very smart and very worried. Their saucer eyes allow them to see 340 degrees, with the capacity to both look behind and see ahead. Remember when you had a teacher who said she had eyes in the back of her head? Well, in a way a horse does. It can take in what's happening behind it, or sense movement behind it, as much as it can take in what's in front of it. Horses have two blind spots, one in the front and one in the back, but otherwise their view of the world is far wider than ours.

What they can't see is anything very far away. If we have 20-20 vision, horses have 20-30—that is, they see something at 6 metres as we would see it at 9 metres. When they look further away, they can see something moving out there on the horizon, but they can't see exactly if it's something good or something bad. That's why objects floating in the sky like paragliders or hot-air balloons worry horses. And why they sometimes can't see something close up until they're right on it. So you might be riding by a mailbox you've been seeing for the last three minutes as you approached it, and your horse suddenly shies away in terror. That's because the horse didn't see it from a distance, and suddenly it's there.

I had a horse named Bolt who was just like that. He was beautiful, big and black, with amazing movement and a big jump—the kind of horse who just oozed X factor. But if he was trotting along and suddenly saw the mailbox next to him? Why, you would have thought the world had ended. All the energy that enabled him to jump or run circles round the ring was suddenly all focused on getting away from the very scary mailbox.

In thinking like a horse it's good to try to imagine what they're seeing in the world around them: if you see things from their point of view, you'll develop a greater under-standing of them. We always assume other animals see the colours of the world the way we do, and they adjust to light and dark the way we do. There have been some pretty interesting studies of this, and it's been found that horses are similar to people who are red–green colour-blind. They know those colours are there, because they seem different from other colours around them, but they don't really see red, and they definitely don't see red when it's on top of green. So a horse is really glad to have the shiny red apple you've brought because it tastes fantastic, but it's not actually taking in that the apple is red. To the horse it's more of a muted autumn brown.

That can mean trouble when you and your horse are out for a ride on an autumn day and you're seeing all kinds of things on the ground in the whole array of colours we see, and your horse is sort of seeing it all in shades of green and brown. If something suddenly moves or stands out as different your horse is going to get spooked, because it hasn't seen the difference in the colours to alert it to the idea it should pay attention. So it gets caught off guard, and then what's it going to do? Worry.

In thinking like a horse it's good to try to imagine what they're seeing in the world around them: if you see things from their point of view, you'll develop a greater understanding of them.

With those enormous eyes of theirs, too, horses adjust to light and dark completely differently from the way we do. Horses evolved out there on the rolling open landscape— steppes and plains and meadows and veldts—in different places all over the world. We humans, and our other ape relatives, developed in forests. Our eyes needed to make adjustments really quickly between light and dark. When you walk into a room after being outside in the sun, there's a minute or two when your eyes haven't made the adjustment to the light and you might be groping in the dark, and then suddenly your eyes have adjusted and you can see relatively well. We never even think about it, unless we're wearing the kind of glasses that are light-sensitive and they haven't caught up with the change yet.

When a horse has been out in the light it can take up to half an hour for its eyes to adjust to darkness: if you live outdoors in the open landscape all the time, sunset and sunrise don't happen like a light switch going on or off. It's a slow thing, and horses' brains and eyes are wired for the slow change of light. They adjust bit by bit to the change while still taking in any potential movement out at the edges of their vision. What better time of day for predators to hunt them than dusk or dawn? So their eyes need to adjust to the change slowly.

But now we bring them into our world. In one way, if you're bringing them into a stable for the night, you're giving them a feeling of safety, because they know nothing's going to get them in there. On the other hand, if they've come into the stable too quickly, their eyes may be struggling to adjust to the darkness. If it's become a familiar space, that's fine, as the smells and the feel of the space will be something the horse knows. If it's entering that space for the first time, though, the horse is going to need time just to be able to see what's happening.

A horse float is even more challenging, and over the years much of my work has been with horses who have been terrified of getting into a trailer or a float. An additional challenge, as well as the way they respond to light, is our lack of knowledge of their past experiences. Horses don't come with a log book, though they do sometimes show visible scars from highly charged encounters. Most of the time, though, you don't know what the previous owners have been like and how many traumatic experiences the horse might have been through.

Horses have amazing memories, especially when it comes to revisiting a place where something very frightening or physically painful has happened to them, and naturally they don't want to repeat that experience. I always let the horses tell me what they know, and they do. An owner may be able to give me a fair bit of their history, but the horses can give me a more honest account in the way they react to the things I do.

So picture the scene at the float. If the horse actually needs half an hour for its eyes to adjust from bright light to darkness, imagine how it feels when it is led really quickly into a float for the first time. While some owners think the horse is just being stubborn by holding back, it might actually be showing its intelligence by being cautious. It truly can't see there's nothing to fear in there.

To make the situation worse, often the owner is looking at his watch because he needs to get on the road. He hasn't taken the time to make sure the horse feels safe or comfortable with the experience, and you can guess what happens. The owner gets angrier and angrier with the horse for holding him up and being what he sees as stubborn and difficult. The horse, feeling the owner's frustration, becomes even more frightened. Because it is already afraid, and the person who is supposed to lead it safely is angry with it for some unknown reason, suddenly it is rearing up and doing everything it can to avoid getting into the float.

After a couple of rounds of that I usually get a call from the frustrated and angry owner, or sometimes the worried and sad owner. I see this all the time. Where knowledge ends, violence starts. Next moment it's 'You bloody bastard, get in the damn float,' and the whips come out. The terrified horse goes in, but it's a time bomb in there and it won't be long before it goes off.

What kind of life is that for a horse? I hope those of us who work with horses will start to see the world from their perspective. The more we learn about why they do what they do, and why they think the way they do, the better equipped we will be to guide them through life.

I have worked with over 7000 horses in the last 25 years and thousands of them have had issues around floats. Most won't go in, some won't come out, but either way, floats are a place where owners and their horses often have problems.

SO LET'S GO BACK to Beanie, the horse who was rearing up at the beginning of this chapter, and really having trouble around floats.

When I first start to work with a horse like Beanie, I try to assess what he is attempting to say through his actions. I ask myself, 'Is he scared? Is he trying? Is this just a big dose of attitude? Is the problem that he's not comfortable in there?'

Initially I worked on getting Beanie in the float, but I kept coming back to the fundamental issue that he just wasn't comfortable in there. He had probably been forced into floats in the past, and I had no doubt he had been bashed around a bit.

The solution in this case involved getting into the float with him, and spending a few hours there working with him.

He would go into the float, but as soon as he looked around at the walls he'd go flying back out. I noticed he would try to only face the front. He trembled and was too scared to look around. He found the sides of the float almost unbearable. The poor fellow just shook and shook.

I came to think he had the leftover memory of a trauma—perhaps he had reared up and hit his head at some time. Whatever it was, it scared him so much that getting close to the wall meant he just wanted to fly out of the float as soon as he got in.

While it's useful to try to work out what might have happened in the past, I never waste too much thought on this. I'd rather spend the time on doing what's needed to get over it. So Beanie and I would both go into the float. I would guide him towards the wall, and when he looked at it I'd give him a rub so he knew it was OK. I repeated the sequence a number of times, and after a while, rather than backing out of the float as soon as he got into it, he decided to trust me to decide when he came out. I would leave him for a bit and then make it my idea to back him out again before he thought of it, so he could receive some praise. We practised this small but very important thing for two hours a day for four days, getting him to the point where he was able to see and touch the walls of the float without being afraid, and with me there to help him calm down. Giving him all this time to become truly happy in the float made all the difference, and in my experience this is always the case.

After four days of working that way I was standing in there with him, helping him to become happy and relaxed, when he did something I will never forget. He looked at me straight on, then he gave a prolonged look at the wall, then he looked back at me for a rub. In his language, what he was saying was, 'Hey, Andrew, look at me! I can look around in here without being afraid.' From then on, Beanie never had any trouble in the float.

What was important here was spending time with him, noticing what the core issue was, breaking down the steps to help him overcome his challenges, then putting them back together. Too many people become impatient and end up doing battle with their horses because they haven't really given them the time to get comfortable. Not long ago I was talking to a friend who had called me in to help her with getting her horse onto the float. She told me something useful that probably applies to a lot of owners. She said, 'You took twice as long to get the horse into the float as I had thought it "should" take the first time. But when you explained why and that by doing this slowly in the early stages we'd have a better result later, I really understood. You have a different kind of confidence about outcomes and how long it takes to get to them, and once I saw that, I could relax more and work with my horse better.' It was as if I was giving her permission to take her time and follow the horse's lead.

If we want to get the best from our horses, the more we understand how they operate, the more knowledge we have in our toolkit, the better equipped we are to help them. I think it also helps to be aware that horses remember trauma. It's really amazing how forgiving they are, considering how badly treated many have been and how long their memories are.

I think their forgiving nature is one of the real positives of developing relationships with horses—we can always try again.

As I've said, horses live with some level of worry all the time. This can be a good survival tool, as it means they remain wary and pay attention to what's happening around them. But if they have had an experience where they have been pushed into a situation that is frightening, like Beanie had been, the next time they encounter that situation they will not only worry, they'll also do everything in their power to avoid it. Avoidance is a favourite tool of horses, and they use it really well. When avoidance doesn't work, though, and we put more pressure on them, this can make them panic and flee, which becomes a lot more dangerous for us. So it's our job to release some of the worry they carry, and to build their confidence so they go through life happier.

Avoidance is a favourite tool of horses, and they use it really well.

When working with horses I'm assessing their emotional state all the time. It's a lot like parenting, or teaching, where you have to put the time in and notice the little things and correct them on a daily basis. Some horses may step right into the float, but when they come out, they fly out of there. I want those horses to have really good manners—they should be able to walk both onto and off a float and be relaxed in both situations.

I do it gradually. One step in, one step back. Another step in and then a pause, a 'Let's see'. If I ask a horse into a float and it backs off, it's telling me it's not happy in there. Another step in and it might back off, but not back all the way out. Now maybe it will step forward to another spot and stand still. It's letting me know it's comfortable there and we can continue. I'm checking its whole being all the time—not only where it is stepping, but if the horse is shaking with fear as Beanie was, or if it's relaxed. I never think about whether the approach we're taking is fast or slow, but about what is appropriate for that horse's worry level.

I do pay attention to whether or not the horse is trying. It's possible to waste a lot of time with a horse who isn't trying and if that's the case, we need to do something to change it. I like horses to be able to stand in the float for a good five minutes without feeling the need to come back out again; only then would I say the horse is comfortable in there.

I do pay attention to whether or not the horse is trying. It's possible to waste a lot of time with a horse who isn't trying and if that's the case, we need to do something to change it.

Once the horse is in the float, and the chain or the bar is up, I want to make sure it has learned to be comfortable with that, too. I play around with the chain so the horse can hear it and become familiar with the sound. So once a horse has learned how to move into the float gradually, it'll also learn to stay still in there until it's asked to come out. Too many horses go flying out of the float, and how is that safe for the people around it? By bringing them into the float gradually, by taking steps in and steps out, they learn there's no need to run in or run out. It can all be done in a calm way.

One of the justifiable fears horses have is that if they walk into a float and it takes them away, they may never come back. We may know we're just going down the road or to a race, but do they?

Early in my career I worked with a team at Windsor Park Stud in Cambridge. We worked with a lot of yearlings, getting them ready for the annual Karaka sale, a top operation run by great people. Those horses walk onto a horse truck, and some never see a paddock again. They're really only like babies at one year old, too. Some go onto a plane and are off to Hong Kong or Singapore where they will be stabled for the rest of their lives. Some get broken in. Some go back to a paddock, but not to the paddock where they began. Some are sold and left in a stable and they have no idea what's going to happen to them next. So they could go into a float and then come out in some place that is completely different from anywhere they've ever been before. They might never go back to what had been home, never see their companions again.

They really are pretty trusting of us. I don't think we give them enough credit considering that for many, their early experiences of floats changed their lives forever.

ONE OF THE FIRST times I ever got some feedback suggesting I had something different or a little special with horses was when I led a frightened horse onto a horse truck. Grand-father was a man who kept his thoughts to himself. He was old-fashioned in that way, I guess. I wanted to learn and he was the person who first introduced me to horses, but he was always really busy running the farm. Like any boy, I would have liked a little praise, and I felt like I was doing a really good job looking after Bobby and Comet, but it wasn't his generation's way.

My younger brother, Nick, and I often stayed with our grandparents, and across the road there was a riding academy with an old S track where the trekking horses would go up and over the hill beyond. The first thing we'd do every morning was pull back the curtains to watch the horses being mustered. I couldn't take my eyes off those horses—I had a huge yearning to be around them and to learn as much as I could.

One day when I was about fifteen, I was riding down the road on Comet and I noticed there were a lot of people milling around in the horse-trekking yard. In the carpark there was a big horse truck from Majestics, which is the largest transporter of horses in New Zealand. The driver was trying to get a horse on board and he wasn't having any luck at all. The horse was just wild, flying backwards and refusing to go anywhere near the truck. One of the people from the trekking outfit, who knew me from my riding around the farm, called out, 'Andrew, can you get this horse on?' I said I'd give it a go, and the guy handed the lead rope over to me. He had clearly been trying for a while and was ready to take a break.

It must have taken me ten minutes, but I calmed the horse down. So much depends on our energy with horses, and I knew my own energy was quiet. When a horse is as hyped up as he was, they just don't think straight. So I just stood with the horse, gave him a few rubs, and spoke quietly to him. After what the horse had just been going through, this quiet approach quickly built some trust between us. Then, much to everyone's amazement, the horse just walked straight into the truck.

I could see my grandfather peering through the hedge watching. Everyone clapped, and I was just really glad I had been able to help. The next day we were having lunch on the farm and out of the blue Grandfather said, 'You did a good job yesterday getting that horse on the truck.' I almost fell off my chair—I'd never heard anything like it from him before. But that one small bit of praise probably did more than anything else to reassure me that I was on the right track. I loved the thought of Grandfather peering through the hedge, too, not wanting to be seen, but still wanting to see what I was doing.

When I'm working with a horse, it's reading my body language all the time, and I am constantly reading what it is saying back. There are a few cues that are big giveaways about how a horse is feeling and how it is going to react to working together. It's not that different from reading people by their body language, as some of the cues are the same. The first one goes back to the eyes. Horses use eye contact as a way of saying they are listening and paying attention to you. Where the horse is looking is usually where it's thinking about going next, so when I work with a horse, I want its attention on me. If I don't have that, I don't have anything.

When I'm working with a horse, it's reading my body language all the time, and I am constantly reading what it is saying back.

Just like a teenager who wants to avoid you, even when you're standing face to face a horse will turn its head and look the other way if it wants to avoid you. It might be looking over your shoulder, suddenly intent on a clump of grass on the ground, or having a good look at its mates over the other side of the fence. It's all conveying that the horse is trying to avoid engaging. That horse doesn't get any praise.

Praise is what the horses I work with really want. Beneath the praise is something that helps them to relax their nervous systems and takes away their worry. They know if they can trust me to lead them, they don't have to be on high alert. They come to like the feeling of trust, knowing what I say is what I mean, that the consistency of my engagement with them is something they can rely on. I'm not some moody bastard who is Mr Friendly one day then yelling at the horse for exactly the same thing the next. Horses crave emotional consistency and knowing they can rely on you to be who you say you are.

But how do you teach a horse to have that trust? Praise. When a horse is doing what I've asked of it, I praise it with words and with touch. I rub the horse in the one place it can't see at all, right between its eyes, on its broad forehead. Most horses love to be touched there, and when a horse has given me its attention and done what's been asked of it, it gets words and lots of rubs. I liken it to a work situation with humans. If someone at the office tells you all the time, 'Good job . . . well done . . . that was great,' you will start to feel pretty good about yourself and your confidence will be high. The same is true of a horse—it will want to try for you.

The first thing I ask of a horse when I'm working with it is to look at me and pay attention. So there's no praise for looking over its shoulder at its mates to see what they're doing, and there's no praise for pretending I'm on a different planet when I'm half a metre away. If I've asked a horse to do something and it's off in its own little dream world, it's not going to receive praise.

Horses are really social animals and they pick up on all of this fast. In a way, they're testing you. And I can't blame them, especially the horses I meet. With the exception of horses who are being broken in for the first time, or who have grown up with very little human contact, most have a whole history of bad experiences around inconsistency that they're bringing to this first encounter. So if their owner or the person who looks after them hasn't required them to make eye contact and to be fully present when things have been asked of them, they don't know this is basic good manners.

I think about this a lot in my work with troubled kids, too. If they've been able to get away with not making eye contact when they meet someone, or have been allowed to be disrespectful, they will use it as a wall to protect themselves until they feel they can trust someone. In time—and this goes for horses as well as people—the walls come down if they are consistently met with the same expectation of good behaviour as well as with praise that recognises they've done what was asked of them.

Many horses suffer from a lack of confidence around humans. I see it both in the horse's body language and the ways in which it might cope with eye contact. Horses aren't used to our intensity. So sometimes we can be working really hard with a horse, and when we stop to give it a break it might look away and avoid us for a while because it's needing some time out. That horse is saying to itself, 'Aw hell, if I look at Andrew he's going to ask me to do something else, so I'll look here and there and anywhere else so I can just relax for a while.'

After a while the opposite starts to happen, too. Often when a horse has been involved in demonstrations it can develop a love of the limelight. Suddenly it's, 'Oh, I've been so good today; don't you think I've been so good?' People come up and want to say hello to the horse after the demonstration, and the horse will go from person to person soaking up the praise, loving being the centre of attention. There are horse divas, too.

In the horse world you might hear the expression, 'Don't look a horse in the eye.' I don't agree with this, but it is essential to look at the horse in the right way. If you're looking at it threateningly, of course you're going to scare it more and make it want to move away. I want to be able to look where I need to look, but I pay very close attention to the horse's eye to see whether it has a harder or softer look in it with regard to the training we're doing.

As I see it, we're working together, perhaps in a sort of coach–player relationship, so my very first step in working with a horse is making sure it knows that when we work together, we make eye contact. A horse who is looking at me when I'm talking to it is a horse who's paying attention, and that horse gets praise.

And who wouldn't like to hear they're doing a great job? I know I sure do.

Reading a horse's body language

RAZZ AND RHYTHM
IN THE WIND

Sometimes, even though they're doing everything right, horses will get themselves into situations where they need your help. Razz was one of those horses, and on this particular day he was in a tangle. He had got his foot stuck in a fence and the wire had become wedged between his hoof and his shoe.

Razz had come to me from the Kapiti Vaulting Club. He was a big grey station-bred horse from Gisborne. On his arrival at the club, he had sent the first person to ride him flying into the dirt, so he'd been brought to me for some re-education. He had been with me for a while and had been doing well.

At the time my partner and I had 25 horses on our farm north of Wellington, and every night it was my job to rug and feed all those horses. Razz was in the first paddock and normally he would have come straight away when his paddock mate came out for dinner, but on this night he stayed down on the fenceline. I figured I'd make my rounds and come back to him when I was done with all the others.

It took a while, but when I came back Razz was still down on the fenceline. He called out to me, and when I went down, there he was with the fence wire running between his hoof and the shoe. Some horses might have panicked and cut their legs to shreds, but what I loved about Razz was that he thought about his situation. He had been leg-roped during his early starting, which would have taught him how to be calm when his leg had to be lifted. As a result of his clear thinking, and probably his trust in me, knowing I would come to help him, he waited calmly until I arrived and was able to free him with some wire cutters.

It's not always easy to know what a horse is thinking, but some of their body language gives us clues if we know to look for them. In Razz's case, his calmness told me a lot about what he was thinking. Afterwards I'm sure he was relieved. I know I was, as he could easily have broken his leg trying to free himself.

Horses wear their thinking, and certainly their mental exertion, on their faces. Often this is clearly visible with racehorses when they come in from the track—the veins in their faces stand out because they have been exerting themselves really hard. When I've done an hour's session with a horse on the ground where I've been getting it to really think, I'll see the horse standing there and its eyes are soft but the veins are out around its face. The horse hasn't necessarily been exerting itself physically, like a racehorse, but it has been using its brain and really thinking. I have never read anything about this, but I believe that when a horse is concentrating really hard or processing its thoughts, it shows. Even if it is only walking and doing basic groundwork, nothing that exerts too much energy, its face and eyes become softer and more expressive.

Another example is a horse with its ears pinned back. You know it's not a happy horse. It's a horse who is trying to give you pretty much the same face as an All Black in the middle of a haka. Eyes rolling, ears back, with a nasty look on its face—a universal sign for 'Back off!' With their heads being so much higher than ours, it can be pretty damn scary.

To read the body language of a horse, I look for a collection of things where each tells me something about how it is feeling and what's going on in its head. Like anything, when you are learning, you have to stop and think. But the more time you spend around horses, the faster you can read and understand what they are saying. With eye contact, if the horse is looking at me it's letting me know it's paying attention. By reading the horse's ears, I can understand the direction of its attention, and work out where that attention is focused.

Like their eyes, horses' ears are different from ours. Our ears just stick out on the sides of our heads, and catch the sound on either side of us. They can't do half the things horses' ears can do. Perched on top of their heads instead of on the sides, horses' ears can swivel almost 180 degrees. They can move almost like an old-fashioned tracking radar, taking in the sound in front of them, or on the side, or behind. Having evolved as prey animals, they needed a pretty big collection of tools to tell them if there was something creeping through the tall grass behind them. Because they have to lower their heads to eat, they might need to be listening to what's ahead of them at the same time as what's behind them, to make sure they have all the territory around them covered.

The more time you spend around horses, the faster you can read and understand what they are saying.

While some people can wiggle their ears, that's really about the extent of what humans can do. Horses' ears, on the other hand, can move separately and can rotate in concert or individually. If you're looking at a paddock of horses you might notice some of them have one ear facing forward and one ear facing back.

So horses are always talking to us in their own way. The more we can read and understand them, the safer we will be around them. When I'm working with a horse I am always taking note of what its ears are doing, as it gives me a gauge of what state the horse is in. If, for example, I am in close at one side, I want that ear tuned into me, so the horse always knows I am there. If I am standing in front, two ears pricked forward towards me means the horse is giving me its full attention. Sometimes there might be one ear forward on me, and one ear on other things that are going on, maybe behind it. Two ears pinned back with a nasty-looking face is not the look I am after—it means 'Look out!' In that situation I usually say, 'Don't pull that face on me!'

What I don't like is when someone is riding a horse and the two ears are pricked forward. It tells me all of the horse's attention is forward, with nothing back on whoever is in the saddle. A great horse to work with is one who is watching and listening. That horse isn't going to get startled or caught offside, whatever happens, because it has the habit of paying attention to the person in its company.

When I'm talking to a horse, I use my quiet speaking voice, and a horse who's tuned in will be listening and wanting to know what we're going to do next. Every time the horse has listened really well, especially when we've just started working together, I praise it, so it knows it has done the right thing.

To me, praising a horse often and specifically, combined with the release of pressure, is the best way to establish clarity in communication. Because we don't speak the same language, if the horse does what has been asked of it, I want it to know the communications between us are working well.

Praise, in the form of touch and tone of voice, is a consistent way of communicating the horse has clearly understood and that I'm really happy with its progress.

To me, praising a horse often and specifically, combined with the release of pressure, is the best way to establish clarity in communication.

Ray Hunt, one of the old American horsemen who helped popularise the notion of natural horsemanship, used to say, 'Reward the smallest change and the slightest try.' I strongly agree with that, and if you do it with a horse you are working with, it knows straight away it is on the right track. For example, if I were teaching a horse to move backwards, the first thing I would do is pick up my energy and start to move that in the horse's direction. If the horse started to prepare, even to shift its weight, I would praise it. Then, next time, if it was just doing that plus the next step, shifting back, I would again praise it, so I communicated very clearly to the horse that it was heading the right way.

If they have asked a horse to do something and it hasn't responded well, many people just think 'dumb horse', but what they should really do is ask themselves if they've communicated clearly enough. Horses don't know what we want from them unless we tell them. Horses are very smart, and if we communicate in an effective and clear way they'll learn very fast. I find it's the same with teaching people. I always try to explain things in the form that's easiest to understand, and if somebody's still not getting it, it's my problem. I might need to be able to explain that one thing in ten different ways until they do get it.

Horses don't know what we want from them unless we tell them.

Not all horses listen from the beginning, and often it's necessary to use reverse psychology to encourage them to choose a different path to the one they began with. Reverse psychology (which also works on people, I hear) is based on the idea of continuing to give the horse a choice, but making their choice harder and harder, until the horse's solution starts to seem like a bad option and my solution starts to seem like a much better one. Ultimately, the horse chooses the better option, and because he has chosen it himself, he owns it. Horses who have struggled with communication in the past, or haven't received very much praise, or praise that is clearly linked to positive reinforcement of behaviour, respond all the more to reverse psychology.

A couple of years back I was working with a horse named Rhythm in the Wind, one who really benefited from this approach. This was when I was still based north of Wellington, so by the time Rhythm arrived from Auckland he'd been in the horse truck for a fair while. We had a yard set up and there were horses all over it, and a little white donkey named Hontis down at the end. I walked Rhythm off the truck, planning to take him down to get a health check on the other side of the yard to the hosing bay. He was about halfway across the yard when he saw this little white donkey and was suddenly completely terrified. Here he was, this huge strong horse, and at just the sight of that little white donkey he was beside himself with fear.

Rhythm suddenly flew backwards and took off, dragging me 20 metres down the laneway. When he finally stopped I tried to get him calmed down, but every time he looked over at that donkey it was as if the world had ended! It was pretty clear to me this horse wasn't really trying to get a grip on himself. He would take a step and then there would be a whole lot of this horse-drama version of him saying, 'Oh, no! Oh no! This is all too terrifying!'

It took me a good twenty minutes to get him into the hosing bay, which was only 20 metres from the truck. I backed him up, and eventually got him there. I understood he was scared, but what bothered me was that he wasn't making any effort to get beyond his fear. And in those first five minutes, I learned that was how Rhythm was with everything. He was telling me just as much about his attitude as he was about his actual concerns. Whatever we were doing in the time I worked with him, if something took two hours with most horses, it took ten hours with Rhythm.

He had clearly been thrashed in the past, and had immediately stopped trying when people took to him with a whip. So he was actually quite clever. He had learned how to communicate his feelings by not engaging. I'm naturally very patient, which you have to be to get the best out of a horse like him, but he was frustrating. He was like a person who would get bored easily and then start to make his own fun. And he clearly didn't suffer fools well.

Most of the time he made me laugh. I'd be walking him down the road on a beautiful sunny day with everyone happy and he'd come and give me a little nip. In response to his nip, I'd back him down the road 100 metres. Then for no reason at all he'd do it again a while later, and we'd back up again. With Rhythm, though, I could back him up 500 metres, which most horses would find terribly hard, and then ten minutes later he would go and do something else he shouldn't. It was as if he had been sent to test me. These are the horses I love working with. They really make you think.

When the young women who worked for me rode him round the racetrack, trotting a couple of laps, he would just stop and stand still. They'd be calling out to me to try to get him to go. Sometimes they had been there for ten minutes trying things, and he would just stand there with a funny look on his face. I would come down and we would all be laughing—it was hard not to. He was just saying, 'No, sorry. I've done a lap.' So what I'd do is try some reverse psychology with him. If he wouldn't move forward, well, I guess we'd go backwards until going forward seemed like a much better idea. He was a horse who took a long time to try at all, as he'd learned that if he didn't try, he didn't have to do much. As I've said, most horses are pretty smart, and Rhythm seemed to have figured it all out! The problem for Rhythm, though, was I had figured *him* out.

PEOPLE OFTEN ASK ME how I know when to get firmer with a horse. The answer really has to do with whether or not they are trying. Sometimes when you ask a horse to do something you'll see they are blatantly looking the other way, not even remotely thinking about what you want. So then you need to act pretty smartly, otherwise you are just wasting your time. If a horse isn't trying, you need to act fast to change it, so you can move forward.

One of the ways in which horses communicate with us is how they hold their heads. A horse who is holding his head up high is telling us he is on high alert. The ideal is a nice low head position, which tells me the horse is relaxed. If I am re-educating a bucking horse, I am constantly looking at the position of his head and reading what he is thinking about the things I'm doing and if he is comfortable. A lot of people will climb aboard a really tense horse and then wonder why they come off. It comes down to not reading or sometimes not caring about what the horse is saying. Horses are highly strung, and many exist in a state of high tension. It's important to release that tension. I always aim to be relaxed, which helps them relax, but I also remain alert to whatever might happen next.

When I begin to work with a horse, the temptation for it is to lean in to the pressure. What does that mean? Rather than trying to release the pressure, a horse who is leaning in to it will deliberately make itself heavy and slow. When a horse is trying to push someone over, standing too close, practically on top of them, it is leaning in to the pressure.

Rhythm, who would resist doing much of anything apart from just standing there like a concrete wall, was the poster-horse for leaning in to pressure. It was pretty clear he had gone through life using his strength to get out of things. But I am just 80 kilograms against his 650–700 kilograms, so how do I get control of a horse like that? I have to soften him up to pressure so he responds to the lightest touch. This is why I do a lot of work with horses on the ground. If they are heavy on the ground, they will be the same under saddle—heavy to steer and horrible to stop. There are many reasons why a horse might shut down or be unresponsive, everything from lack of education to mistreatment in the past.

What I want to develop is the capacity to move the horse without any touch at all, and to get an immediate response. So every time I work with a horse, I am looking for a quicker and softer response; that way we are always moving forwards with the horse.

If a horse is holding its head really high when we meet, I will also teach it to drop its head. The way I teach this is by having one hand on the lead rope, keeping the horse's head straight, then putting my other hand just behind the top of the head collar and using my thumb and second finger to apply pressure. It doesn't have to be much—a horse can feel a fly on its back. Most horses will try to go against the pressure to start with, but the pressure remains, so then they have to think about how to release it. As soon as a horse drops his head, the pressure is gone, and he soon starts to work out the connection. The key is to respond quickly and release the pressure as soon as he drops his head.

What I want to develop is the capacity to move the horse without any touch at all, and to get an immediate response.

I also use this when I'm teaching my horses to accept the bridle. First I get them to the point where they respond really quickly to that super-soft head pressure. Then, when they're ready for the bridle, I hold the bit in my left hand and put my right hand up between the horse's ears. With some very light pressure from my forearm, I drop the horse's head down to accept the bridle properly before opening its mouth, putting the bit in, then slipping the bridle over the ears. This is especially useful with big horses, as it means they come down to my height, rather than me having to reach up on my toes.

If a horse is slow to respond to that pressure and release, we work on it over and over again until eventually the horse starts to comprehend the relationship between the two. I know most people who work with horses believe the release of pressure is the reward for the horse, but I think it's more subtle than that. I think the release of pressure, the correct response from the horse, and then immediate praise become linked in the horse's mind so it understands it will be praised when it responds quickly to a request. The fact that the pressure is released at the same time is an added benefit, but not the motivation.

The way a horse tells me it's starting to feel relaxed is to give a big sigh. Often when I'm giving a demonstration with a horse, the moment when the horse lets out a sigh is the same moment when the whole audience, who have been unconsciously holding their breath, also start to relax. They sigh almost in tandem with the horse, and then people just start laughing. I might just smile a little myself, too. It's a great sound, both from the audience and from the horse. When I hear the horse give that big sigh I know it is starting to relax and let go of some of the tension inside it.

When I hear the horse give that big sigh I know it is starting to relax and let go of some of the tension inside it.

Another thing I always look for when training horses is the licking of the lips. Often out in the paddock, when you see a young foal or a horse meeting older or bigger horses, you will see it chewing and licking its lips. What it is saying here is, 'I'm only little. Don't hurt me.' But it's also a sign they are starting to get the things we are teaching them. Some horses don't do it very much, or they make you work fairly hard for it, while others can be very expressive and lick all the time.

I often see it when we're working on float loading. When the horse is in the float for a while, I'm waiting for it to adjust and feel happy. After a while, it will have a lick of its lips. Then, maybe ten minutes later, another lick, then another, say, five minutes later, and maybe two minutes after that one, followed by a big sigh as they finally let go and soften.

The way horses use their mouths is also really interesting. You often see horses who have learned how to pick up another horse's feed bucket once they realised their paddock mate might be getting a different and better mix. Or you hear stories of horses who have learned how to turn the water tap on (but strangely, not off) if they want a drink. When horses discovered how easy it was to open up their gates and let themselves out, different gate latches had to be invented. My horse Rock used to get all antsy when he was left in the covered yards. He'd spend all his time trying to figure out how to open those latches, or he might jump the gate. I always used to joke that if there was a fire in the barn I didn't have to worry, Rock would be fine. In fact, he'd probably come and get me out of bed!

Many owners who have affectionate relationships with their horses have had the horse put its head over their shoulder and take a nibble on a button on their shirt, or take a bite out of the apple they were eating.

JUST AS WE ARE always trying to learn as much as we can about a horse from its body language, it's reading ours, too. I don't know if horses read us from our eyes, ears, mouths, and the way we hold our heads, as we read them. I'd love to read the book they might write about 'human whispering'. They certainly are able to read the most subtle aspects of our energy, and they respond to it all the time. It's one of those aspects of relationships with horses that can be rewarding for everyone. They really notice.

If you've had a bad day, your horse can feel your energy. If you've had a really great day, your horse can feel your energy. If you've just had a huge blow-out with your partner, your horse can feel it before he even sees you. If you're feeling lonely and there's no one in the world who gets you, your horse will read it in your shoulders and the way you walk out to the paddock. Throughout my life, when I've been at my lowest, my horses have always known it. And when I've been at my best, they've known it, too. Rock, my old guy, he knows it all. He's 24 now, and he's one of my best friends. Maybe it's good he can't tell anyone all the stories he knows about me.

One of the best things about those big eyes horses have is that they can reflect back to us who we are. Sometimes we might think that's a gift and sometimes we might think it's a burden, but to horses, what they want when they look at us never really changes. They want to be understood. They want their language to be understood. It's pretty simple really. If we want to get the best from them, it's important to learn why they do what they do. We need to be able to read them and see things from their point of view if we are to develop our relationship with them and get the outcomes we want.

Everything else is carrots and apples. But when it comes down to it, what they want most is for us to care about their happiness, just like we care about all of the people we love. It's that simple. Training horses is not rocket science. It just demands a good healthy dose of common sense. But as humans, we don't always apply it.

And more often than not, that's when I get called in.

Horses as social animals

PERCY AND BRAVE

One of the most impressive people I've worked with is a woman named Thea Griffin. We first met when I was studying in Australia, and later I worked for her on her property outside Melbourne. Thea is an amazing horse-woman, and I learned so much from her. One of the many stories she told me was about a mare who taught a young stallion the value of proper behaviour in the band. According to Thea, while many people believe that in the wild the stallion is the boss, it's actually the lead mare who is really in charge.

One day, Thea told me, she was watching a group of horses where there was a cocky youngster, a one- or two-year-old, who had become very disrespectful and had started picking on some of the older mares, kicking out at them and trying to throw his weight around. The lead mare of the herd watched him for a while, then when she had seen enough she charged the youngster and drove him from the group. Banished from the band, he would struggle to look after himself well, or for long, especially if the threat of predators was high. So, of course, he tried to come back to the herd. As he nonchalantly tried to return, the lead mare faced him, staring him down once again. He stood there, head lowered, knowing he couldn't come back.

That mare, she was tough. She left him out on his own for two or three hours. At some stage, she must have thought he had learned his lesson, so she gave him the signal in horse language that he was welcome again. She turned her shoulder, and with that she invited him back in. So the youngster came in, and he was good for perhaps ten or fifteen minutes. But it didn't take long before he was right back into his old behaviour, so the mare charged him again and left him out there for another few hours. This time he must have learned something, because when the mare dropped her shoulder and invited him back in again, he behaved.

It's that sort of experience of watching horses in the wild that teaches us about how they interact with each other and how we can be better at engaging with them, too. A horse who can't get on with others may need some 'time out' to think about its actions or behaviour, like this young one did.

Once he had learned his lesson, he was welcomed back into the band. The threat of banishment can be powerful, reinforcing that antisocial behaviour won't be tolerated, whether it's in a human band or a horse one.

A horse who can't get on with others may need some 'time out' to think about its actions or behaviour.

Learning about how horses interact socially not only helps us make sense of their behaviour with each other, but is also interesting in terms of how we have interacted with horses in the course of our long history with them. While no one seems to know exactly when horses were first ridden by people, one educated guess I've heard puts it at about 5000 years ago. Images of horses have certainly been with us for a long time, often drawn on the walls of caves, so people have certainly been studying them, looking at them and thinking about them for a long time—more than 30,000 years.

Horses have played a huge part in changing human lives, which is something I think we often forget today. It wasn't that long ago that horses were our main vehicles, whether as fast thoroughbred Lamborghinis or as poor old drays who pulled the family wagon. They've been the hard labour behind a farmer ploughing a field, and they've been used as the basis of mail services across huge areas of the world. Wars have been won on the backs of horses, and the history of whole cultures, such as those of the Native Americans, changed when one tribe had horses and the other didn't.

Horses have also been loyal companions and partners to humans in a way no other animals except dogs have been. For the most part, people love their horses and establish good, long-lasting relationships with them. In my work I tend to see a lot of people who don't have these relationships, and it helps to understand why that is. I think one of the main reasons is that a lot of the things we think we know about horsemanship have come to us from a time when horses were mainly work animals. Their purpose was to do what we needed them to do, and quickly, and if we didn't get our way through persuasion we would get it by force. Thinking about the horse's happiness would have been like considering whether or not your car is happy. You just want it to start and get you where you want to go.

Many people mistreat their horses not because they intend to, but because they have received really bad advice or training. In New Zealand we have absorbed a range of concepts about horses from the different cultures that make up our country, some of them good and some not so good. The British used their horses for everything from farming to the military and racing, so they brought a whole range of ways of being with horses. We also have traditions from other European countries, which include ideas associated with the military and things like dressage and very formal training from the Polish and Viennese cultures. Then there's the colonial history we share with places like Australia, the US and Canada.

So many of these approaches are based on mastering horses by inflicting pain, or through the promise the pain will stop if the horse will just do as it is told. Horses who don't respond well to this approach use everything they've got to communicate they don't like it, so they become branded as bad horses because they rear up, buck, bite or just won't be 'broken'.

Many people mistreat their horses not because they intend to, but because they have received really bad advice or training.

Ideas have changed over recent years, and I think my generation looks at horses in a different way. I imagine this is probably similar to the way it was when the first people were able to get onto the backs of horses. Despite the ways in which horses have been treated over the last few thousand years, when they are shown respect most horses seem to enjoy their relationships with us as much as we enjoy ours with them. It's mutual. There's something really good happening between us, especially when we're able to communicate well so our horse knows what we're thinking and what we want to do almost as soon as we think it. Then it's like magic.

Most people think horses are herd animals because when they see images of wild horses being mustered it looks like they're in one huge thundering herd. They do live in groups, or bands, but that's different from a herd or a flock. Horses do best in small bands, like family groups, and they move around together within their bands—some young, some older, with both stallions and mares in various places in the social order. It seems that, within these bands, the social relationships between horses are as complicated as, well, our relationships with our friends, families and communities. Imagine that.

The big difference is that horses are prey animals and we're not. We're a mix of everything—sometimes predator, sometimes prey—which is probably why we're all over the show a lot of the time, but it also means some things that are hardwired into horse thinking aren't obvious to us. It helps to remember that no matter what, a horse has a lot of worry.

Horses feel safer in a group. Wild horses need the safety of their group for survival, and they can relax a little more when they are within a band. They are also very intelligent socially, and positions within a band of horses are constantly being tested. Like us, horses look for good leaders, because a leader who is looking out for their band means safety and peace for everyone else. A boss, on the other hand, is just like a boss in our world. We might follow them because we have to, but not always because we want to.

It's remarkable that horses are able to transfer their capacity to feel safe when they are part of a band, and to feel safe under the guidance of a good leader, to humans. Letting us lead them is their incredible gift to us. If we accept their trust and that they're willing to jump across the species fence to be our companions, it's pretty amazing to see the relationships that can develop. That's the part I really love about working with horses.

It's important to understand that this feeling of being part of the band, and having a leader (and sometimes more than one leader), is essential to a horse's happiness. Failing to understand this can lead to many negative horse behaviours. A horse who is left alone in its paddock without any companions will eventually become very depressed. For them, as for us, it's like being put in solitary confinement.

Horses use the threat of abandonment or exile as a way of teaching the young members of their band good behaviour. Sometimes a horse will make the choice to separate itself, but this is usually done under stress. Several years ago I met and worked with a horse who had made that choice, and in the end it couldn't have been more devoted. But not in the beginning.

I MET BRAVE DURING my second trip to Mt Nicholas Station, on the shores of Lake Wakatipu. Brave was a beautiful horse, tall and grey with four white socks and a thin white blaze. While all the horses looked stunning in that land-scape, with the mountains all around them, Brave was especially striking. He looked like one of the glaciers on the top of the mountains. Even before we'd really got into starting them, I had decided Brave was going to be one of the horses I took back to Wellington with me. He was just magnificent.

We had fourteen wild horses to work with, so we had one yard where we could catch them, then I would hand each one to someone else in another yard while we worked with the next one. The yards were at the end of a gravel road, about an hour and a half's drive from the lake. After about five days I had gone through the basics with Brave. I had been able to get him to come off the lead and soften to pressure, move his hindquarters, back up, and he was learning to tie up, but he was still really wild.

All the yards were full that day, and what I should have done was just run him out into the paddock for the day, as he still wasn't ready to be led in an open space. But instead I thought, 'I'll just go around this small gate and I'll lead him into another paddock and let him go.' Well, of course, instead of coming along quietly, he rushed through the gate, then he pulled away and pulled away, and finally he got completely away from me. He ran seven laps around the paddock, his rope flying around him, and I thought, 'Good boy, you've got a brain. You won't do anything stupid like run through a fence.'

Well, the eighth time he came around, he took one look at me, as if to laugh, and then he just leapt over the fence and galloped off. Then, to prove the point, he jumped the next fence too. The rope had swung over his back by now, and I was cursing myself because I was afraid he'd injure himself. I was particularly annoyed as I shouldn't have let this happen. Once Brave jumped that second fence he headed down the gravel road that led to the lake. He took it at a full gallop, jumped the cattle stop, then just disappeared down the road.

It was just before lunch and I was starving, but of course I had to go and find him. I hitched a ride and set out, eventually finding him a full 5 kilometres up the road. He was shaking. I think he had suddenly realised he was completely out of his comfort zone. There was no one around, and in particular no horses, and he had had a hell of a fright. I went up to him nice and easy, took his rope, and he followed me like a lamb all the way home.

At the end of two weeks I took Brave back with me to Wellington, and he went on to become a fantastic demonstration horse. Later, we sold him to a very good horsewoman, Sonya Glennie, whose son rode him. In 2012, just two years from the wild, he placed in the Junior Show Jumper of the Year, then went on to become Reserve Hunter of the Year. Unfortunately, he then had two years out with a leg injury, but he is back in action now with Sonya in the saddle. At the time of writing he was lying second in the New Zealand Amateur Show Hunter Series.

I knew that horse could jump just from what I saw on the station that day, and I've always been glad that after his one fright at finding himself out alone he stayed in our company. It's really important to remember horses are social animals and they need companions. Sometimes a horse who has had injuries or can't be ridden can be kept as a paddock mate for other horses who are more actively engaged. Horses need the mental stimulation of their companions, and if they can't find it among other horses, they'll look for it in humans.

My grandfather had a racehorse, Percy, who was retired up the road in a big 35-hectare hill paddock all by himself. I felt really sorry for Percy, and I would ask Grandfather to let me bring him down to be with the other horses. Grandfather always said, 'Nah, he's fine up there, we don't really need him down here.' But he wasn't fine. He would come barrelling down the hill to see me any time I went anywhere near his paddock. If there was ever a horse who seemed to be calling out, 'Hey, Andrew!', it was Percy. He was about twelve, and he had probably been up there in his paddock for a good five years with just some sheep for company.

It's really important to remember horses are social animals and they need companions.

I would often go up there with some treats and to say hello. Percy had a beautiful attitude and was always so pleased to have me around. I would call and call, and then I would hear him respond, but because the paddock was so big I still couldn't see him. I could hear him coming, though, and all of a sudden he would appear—galloping straight down a steep hill, jumping the creek, and stopping right in front of me. Hello!

He must have been so tough, mentally, that horse. Years later, I ended up looking after him. He came up the coast with me and became the babysitter for my younger horses and clients' horses. He had a great life then, just being himself and getting fed. And just like old times, he still called out to me when it was dinner time.

SO WHY DO HORSES like us at all? One reason is they, like us, are terribly curious. They can't help themselves. When they are feeling safe and not so worried, they want to explore and find all about what's going on. Some are social and are busy paying attention to everyone else, but most are just curious about the world around them.

The youngest horse I have at the moment is a three-year-old whom my son, Luca, has named Cool Guy. Like any three-year-old, he is just into everything. Nothing worries him. He trots or canters along next to the car, gets in the way, licks the car, tries to pull the wiper blades off, stands in front of the truck when I harrow or spread horse poo, and just plays for hours with his group of five mates. He is pretty funny to watch as he plays with one horse for a while, then when that one gets sick of him he's over to see the next horse. If I leave a jersey hanging on the fence, I'll turn around to find him chewing it, or he's pulling rugs off the fence. I figure this is all telling me he's ready to learn and wants to be doing things.

There's a long history of horses who could learn all kinds of unexpected things. In the nineteenth century there was apparently a horse named Clever Hans who everyone believed could do maths. Turned out he couldn't actually do maths, but he could read his owner's expectations so well he could work out the right and wrong answers from his reactions. Today it seems scientists are discovering what people who have worked with horses have known all along. They are just bloody smart, and they want to be thinking and taking in new information all the time.

Horses need stimulation, and spending time and working with your horse is a great way to keep its mind really sharp and active. This is an aspect of the world they inhabit in the wild, and it's just as important for them to have that edge and to be constantly learning when they have become part of our lives. It is especially important today when a lot of horses are kept in small paddocks and off the grass. There isn't much happening for them in their day but lots of boredom and stress at not having grass to graze, so it's really important that we, as owners, get them out and do lots with them.

I use a horse's curiosity all the time to expand the tasks we're going to do together, because most horses want to learn more. Their processing time is different from ours, though. When I want a horse to really learn something, I give it time to process the last experience and the last lesson. I call this 'soaking in' time, and the younger the horse, the longer the soaking in time often has to be. I would rather a horse had more of these soaking in periods and time to think about what we did the day before or what we have just finished, than move it quickly through a whole lot of information. There are no prizes for cramming information into a horse's head—if you really want a horse to understand something, you have to take time and do it over and over until you're sure the horse really has it.

Many people assume too quickly that if a horse has done something once, it knows it. In fact, it may need much more practice before the task is really locked into its knowledge base. Horses learn best through repetition, so I will do something over and over until I'm sure the horse has got it, at the same time varying things so it doesn't get sick of the same thing.

Many people assume too quickly that if a horse has done something once, it knows it.

A lot of owners get quite down at times when their horse has been really silly on a particular day, and they might go home and worry about it all night. Apart from creating a whole heap of issues in this way, the fact is that often the horse will be completely fine the next day. I'm a big believer in just working consistently with the horse, and the results will come.

A horse who moves faster, or is a bit flighty, is also one who is likely to learn more quickly. We can't train a horse if we can't move it, so horses who move easily tend to learn quickly. At the other end of the scale, a horse who is too shut down or hard to move will need more pressure to get it going.

Sometimes in demonstrations you'll see a horse who is particularly flighty. Often the trainer has chosen that horse specially because he or she knows there's no risk of asking it to do something and it just standing there and doing nothing. You sure don't want to be in front of a crowd of people with a horse who has ground to a halt and isn't going anywhere! The only way to get that horse moving would be to increase pressure, and it may not be the best look.

It's a whole combination of things that leads to a horse feeling safe and comfortable, who is completely responsive, who is a thinker and who is keen and ready to please. Because horses are such social and bright animals, there is so much for us each to gain through being in a relationship together, and that's the best part of all. Whether it's the Braves or the Percys in our lives, there is nothing better than being greeted at the gate with a great horse 'Hello!' and to give a big pat and a hello back.

Getting started

PETAL AND BOLT

When I was starting out, I was determined to learn as much as I could about horses and how to work with them. I wanted to learn from good people who would know more than I did.

I had seen a course advertised in my grandfather's racing magazines, a certificate in horse business management at Marcus Oldham, an agricultural college an hour outside Melbourne. They only took four or five New Zealanders each year, so I had no idea whether or not I would be able to get in, but I went up to Auckland for an interview and was accepted. I knew no one and I remember feeling incredibly nervous at the beginning, but in the end I made lifelong friends there. I was just twenty when I started.

The course was one-third business, one-third management and one-third practical. It was designed to open the students' eyes to just about everything in the horse industry, from learning to do injections to getting up early to bring in horses and do track work. We also created business plans and developed marketing strategies. We visited stud farms and even learned to trim feet by pulling horse legs out of a freezer and practising on them.

One of the highlights of the programme was a four-week breaking-in course. It was here I first met Thea Griffin, and right from the beginning I liked everything about what she was doing. The course was led by a guy who was an ex-rodeo rider, who travelled around Australia with his horse truck and trailer, running clinics and breaking in horses. Although some of his methods were in line with the more humane approach of natural horsemanship, he was still a cowboy at heart, and he liked to get on and buck them out. You know by now how I feel about that—even at twenty that was how I felt.

Thea had a much softer approach. She understood the horses and had a quiet confidence about her. I had never broken in horses before, so in a way this was a chance for me to choose between their two styles. One of the reasons I liked Thea's approach was that I wasn't the world's best rider, and she instilled a real sense of safety in people and worked the horses until they were ready to be ridden. I really appreciated that.

There's a perception that the old-fashioned way of breaking in a horse is faster than the modern 'horse whispering' way, but I don't agree with it. The old way is also much harder on the horse.

In the more traditional approach, the people who start the horses 'long rein' them, which means they have the bit in, then reins coming back from the bit. The horses are taught to respond to the reins and to steer before anyone gets on to ride them. The next step is to hobble the horse by tying up one of its legs with leather straps, then sack them out—which means to desensitise them with, for example, plastic bags and ropes. The danger with hobbling the horse—especially if it's a racehorse, as they are often pretty delicate—is they can fall over and break their legs really easily if they're not on all fours.

After this the horse is saddled, and the horse breaker might get up on the horse while he still has one leg hobbled so he can't buck them off. Often the old-timers only had one saddle, which was somehow supposed to fit all horses, so it would have been uncomfortable for the horse, too. The result of all this is that instead of everything being set up smoothly, so the horse never even begins to learn any bad habits, anything can happen.

It wasn't the road I wanted to take, and it seemed to me Thea offered a much better approach. She was using a lot of the new thinking about horses, including Neurolinguistic Programming (NLP), a method that teaches the mind to think more positively, and she made everything she did look effortless.

Thea was probably in her mid-thirties when we first met at Marcus Oldham. She had grown up on an outback station in Queensland—she said it was so big that if you fell off your horse somewhere out on the station it could take you two days to walk back. She told me that one day she was driving back to the homestead when her car broke down. When she couldn't get it going, she looked up to the horizon and called out to one of her horses. When it came to her she climbed onto it bareback, with just an old rope round its chest, and rode it all the way home. That's pretty good as far as I'm concerned—a lot better than the AA.

To get out to the back paddocks of the station for mustering, they'd have to leave at three in the morning. Their horses were tough, really tough. One time, Thea said, her brother was riding one of the big station stallions and they had been riding, trotting and cantering all day. When they finally got home it was six o'clock, and the horse just dropped his head and bucked for half an hour. Imagine being tough enough to work a fifteen-hour day and still have the energy to buck for half an hour, too. That's a tough horse.

Thea had the gift of being an amazing communicator, both with people and with horses. Her stories were always great to listen to, and I learned a lot from them. I loved that she had such a deep connection with her horses. She had two or three horses she could do just about anything with. Her mother, who had died when Thea was twelve, had apparently been a fantastic horsewoman. The horse Thea used for demonstrations was one of the last ones her mother had bred, which would have been really special for her.

ANOTHER COMPONENT OF THE course was a two-week study tour of New Zealand horse farms, and another two-week tour in Australia's Hunter Valley. As a result I was offered a couple of jobs, and after I graduated I came home to New Zealand and worked on a stud farm in Cambridge. There I was working with yearlings, getting them ready for the Karaka sales.

Not long after I came home, though, I wrote to Thea saying I just wanted to learn from her, and I'd be willing to work for nothing. I knew there was a lot more I could learn from her. It was some time later that Thea called to say she had come off a horse and broken her wrist. Did I want that job? I was on the plane back to Melbourne two days later.

Thea and her partner had a property they were developing just outside Melbourne, where she had about 25 horses as well as cattle, sheep, geese and her dogs. I lived in a little tin shed that served as both bunkroom and tackroom. Early on I asked Thea what she had done to promote herself and her business. She replied she had done nothing but work her horses at home then, when she felt they were ready, she took them to a show and won everything there. Then the next weekend she did the same thing again, until everyone in the horse community was saying, 'Wow, where did this woman come from?'

I thought this was a brilliant way to establish a reputation, by showing what you're capable of instead of talking yourself up. I am a big believer you should walk your talk, and it's even better if you don't have to talk at all.

I spent a year with Thea in all. Most of what we did involved starting horses and working with some of Melbourne's worst problem horses. Many of these had been problems for up-and-coming event riders—horses who had bucked their riders off, or had broken people's arms. I finished off some of the horses Thea had started before she broke her wrist. One of the highlights for me was when we went back to Marcus Oldham, where I had first met her, and ran the breaking-in course together. We had 26 students working in pairs to break in thirteen horses. It was only two years since I had been a student there, and now here I was teaching with Thea.

One of the great lessons I learned during this time was from a big Anglo-Arab–Percheron cross named Petal. Percherons are big draught horses—if a horse is even one-eighth Percheron, people often want them for the rodeos because they just have so much power.

Petal was the horse who had thrown Thea when she broke her wrist, and she had been in the paddock ever since. So in a way, I owed my job to Petal. I started working with her the day I arrived and she had been going beautifully. She never bucked, never did anything wrong, and for three months she had been ideal. On this particular Monday we were coming off a weekend course where I rode her all weekend and she was great. I couldn't have been happier with her.

Come Monday morning, Thea said to me, 'Why don't you take Petal for a hack around the road?' I was annoyed at this, because I thought Petal had worked pretty hard over the weekend and should just have the day off. When I went to the paddock to catch her she was just dozing in the sun, all sleepy, and I woke her up. I felt bad about it.

We had an 8-kilometre loop we used to do with the horses. It started out on the farm, then there was a long firebreak all the way down the boundary, so we could take that until we got onto a gravel road. Normally when we rode the horses out it was with plenty of energy, but on this day I just let Petal poodle along half asleep, thinking I was being really kind to her. We were ambling along the firebreak when all of a sudden she woke with a fright and scared herself half to death. I knew there was an electric fence along one side of us, and thought if she touched it we'd be in serious trouble. But even without that she got herself into a tizzy, spinning and spinning us both around before she bucked me off and then cantered off down the firebreak.

Luckily, Thea had seen the whole thing from up at the house, so she jumped in her truck and came down to see if I was OK. We drove down and caught Petal, and afterwards I trotted her for maybe 8 kilometres around the road. She spooked at every letterbox along the way, and I realised she was using the spooking as a way of slowing down, too. It was a form of laziness.

She had been about two weeks away from going home, and I was really gutted. I felt all the good teaching we had done with her had really been for nothing if she was still able to throw me off and be so silly.

I learned a huge lesson from the experience. I had let her get too switched off, and because she was half asleep she got a terrible fright when she woke up. She hadn't remembered I was on her back, so it wasn't much fun for me either. These days I wouldn't say, 'Oh, poor thing, you can rest while we walk.' It's much more important that if we're doing a job the horse needs to be there 100 per cent, tuned in and awake.

If we're doing a job the horse needs to be there 100 per cent, tuned in and awake.

Some horses hold back and then they can explode. Petal was one of those horses, and she taught me about the tension between the two states. Thea had a lot of horses on the farm I'd call 'nutcases', and it was our job to get them right. It was from many of these horses that I learned about the subtleties of horse behaviour, and some of the 'fine tuning' work that's so useful in what I do.

I worked with a lot of different breeds while I was in Melbourne—Quarter horses, Paint stallions, Andalusians, a Morgan horse, Warmbloods, Arabs, loads of thoroughbreds, ponies, standardbreds, and a lot of what they call Australian stock horses.

We had one horse who was an American Saddlebreed, descended from riding horses bred at the time of the American Revolution. There were only a few of these in Australia and this one had been imported from the US. When I first saw him, I thought he had a funny look in his eye—the kind of thing you notice, but you don't always know why. We were riding along in the arena one day when all of a sudden he reared up and started falling backwards. I jumped off the side of him pretty quickly. This was a case where some of the ex-rodeo guys would have got back onto him and ridden him until they had cured him of the behaviour. My approach was to build a relationship so the horse wanted to do anything for me, instead of disciplining it for bad behaviour after the act. So it was with the Saddlebreed—I figured the best way to get a result was to put in the time at the front end of the relationship. By taking things slowly with him, he turned out beautifully and went happily back to his owner.

I had to make sure they would work well with their owner. I wanted all the horses who came my way to have the skills and knowledge to keep themselves and their owners out of trouble.

What I was also finding out was that when I was working with horses for other people, it didn't really matter what I could do with them, I had to make sure they would work well with their owner. I wanted all the horses who came my way to have the skills and knowledge to keep themselves and their owners out of trouble. I needed a system that would erase the horse's problem, and that everyone could follow.

Not all of the jobs involved starting or re-educating horses, though. There were some high ranges across from the farm, and a mountain top where someone wanted to put a big concrete plaque. As is so often the way, the people who wanted the plaque hadn't thought it through before they put in 600 steps leading to the top of the mountain. Now, though they had the steps, they couldn't get anything else up there. So we got a job taking pack horses up the mountain with all the materials they needed. Thea and I each rode one horse and led another one; coming down, we just leaned back as the horses took the steps all the way. It was good fun.

When I was working with Thea I would get up each morning not knowing what was in store for me. One day it might be, 'Andrew, jump on that horse bareback, take a coil of wire and some fence cutters, and ride out over the farm and check the fences.' I'd say, 'What, on *this* horse? It's only had two rides and it can't even steer properly yet.' Thea would just laugh and say, 'Off you go. Good luck!'

It was part of her plan, though, that when I was off doing those jobs I wasn't really thinking about the horse. I was just riding off, looking around with a job to do, and the horses would go with the flow.

Thea was also a big fan of the old free roadside grazing, and every morning we would drive the cattle down the road and leave them in a 2-kilometre strip that was open to roads at both ends. We would always have a different horse we were starting tied up in the yard, and if the cattle came out too close to the road I would canter down and push them back in again. It was good training for the young horses, getting them steering back and forth behind the cows.

Thea was probably the best teacher I've ever had. I always felt really safe when she was around. We would ride out together every day and she would just look at my horse and tell me what to do. She was a master at reading horses, and if she said a horse was ready to ride, it was. Sometimes people say the same thing about me now—just having me there, reading the horse, makes them feel safe. But when I came back to New Zealand and first went out on my own, I really had to test myself for a while, to see if what I thought was right with a horse actually was. I remember thinking, 'I'm going to have to get this right, or I'm going to get hurt.' I didn't have Thea there to tell me what to do anymore.

> **I remember thinking, 'I'm going to have to get this right, or I'm going to get hurt.' I didn't have Thea there to tell me what to do anymore.**

Fortunately, I always got it right. It's something I take pride in now, that after working with thousands of horses I've never had one buck after it went back to its owner. When I said a horse was safe and ready to ride, no one was ever thrown off it. And most of the horses I meet have major bucking problems, or are other 'nutcases', or they are horses who are getting started. It all comes back to reading and understanding them, and building the relationship so they aren't thinking 'Bugger off'. It's about setting things up so the horse is more than ready for what you are asking it to do.

IT WAS 1996 BY the time I came back to New Zealand. I was 23 years old and I wanted to strike out on my own. Initially I lived with my parents, then I went flatting in Wellington. I had always done a lot of gardening work around the district, so I was quite well known and had built up a good reputation. In the beginning, to pay the bills, I used to do gardening work for three-quarters of the day then spend maybe a quarter of my time working on horses. There weren't many people doing this kind of work, so I knew in time I would be able to develop it into a life for myself.

This was when I got Rock and his brother Pamper. I kept them at my grandfather's farm and at the stables across the road, where I traded gardening work for the use of their facilities. While I may not have had a lot of money during that period of my life, I had a lot of time, and the time I put into those horses meant the world to me. Pamper was one of those horses who initially could take an hour to catch, possibly because of my stubbornness in insisting he was going to be caught in the paddock, not run into the yard. In those early days the two of us spent a lot of time learning a whole lot about each other, and I probably developed some finer skills around patience.

A lot of Wellington people grazed their horses in the Ohariu Valley, so I might ride one of my horses up the road and give lessons to two or three people along the way. What a good life in so many ways—to be able to arrive at work on horseback, tie the horse up, do a lesson, then climb back on and ride on to the next one. After a while, I started to take horses in, and work more and more with problem horses.

As I was starting to get more of this type of work, I had a call from a woman who lived up the Kapiti coast. She had bought a big white station horse named Spook, who had bucked his previous owner off, breaking his leg. This woman had fallen in love with Spook, even knowing his history, so she had bought him, brought him home, and what do you know—he bucked her off. The unfortunate thing was that after that she was petrified of him.

So she called me and I went out to have a look at him. In some ways his problem was simple, but it took a wee bit of time to fix. It seemed as soon as someone swung a leg over him he wanted to buck them off. This habit had become pretty ingrained, so I spent hours with him, swinging up, lying over him, and sitting side saddle on him until he eventually came right. The girlfriend I had at the time ended up buying Spook, and she had him all these years until he died in 2015. He was one of those examples of a horse who, once we'd solved the problem, went on to be a great and solid horse.

I learned later that his body was sore, and that he was a horse who needed massage. At that stage I hadn't learned that the first question I needed to ask was whether or not the horse was in pain. Because he was so tough, he didn't let on he was in pain, but in the end we found out and that made a big difference.

Most of the horses I worked with had developed bad behaviours around things like bucking, bolting or rearing. They usually needed re-education work, and sometimes their owners did as well.

Bolt was a beautiful jet-black Clydesdale–thoroughbred cross, though he looked like a thoroughbred. He moved beautifully and had everything, except confidence. If he'd had the personality of some of the other horses who believed they were amazing, I wonder what he could have become, but instead he had a lot of self-doubt. When I met him he was owned by a young woman who had brought him up from the South Island, where he'd been broken in. He was a very highly strung, sensitive horse and she made some big mistakes with him; she was also more interested in partying than putting in time with a young horse. It wasn't surprising he started bucking.

After I re-educated him, he was going beautifully. His owner came for a few lessons but she couldn't put the everyday work into him that he needed, so I ended up buying him. He was a good lesson in how to work with a horse who uses bucking to get his way. As I had with Rhythm in the Wind, who would back up for a long way until going forward seemed like a better idea, I employed a bit of reverse psychology: I used a flank rope to encourage Bolt to buck as much as he wanted without me or anyone else on his back. Using a flank rope desensitises the horse from its belly back to its flanks, and also releases the tension it might be holding in that area. In a way, it was like letting someone with a bad temper just rage and rage until they'd got it out of their system. He quickly learned it was just really hard work running round bucking. Instead, he tuned up his attitude so he was super-keen to please and do the right thing.

Later, Bolt was used by my friend Catarina Strom, the New Zealand vaulting coach. Catarina did a lot of schooling and jumping with him, and in time she could stand up on his back as he was walking around the arena—he would be completely tuned in and looking after her. Bolt went on to win many show hunter competitions and became a pretty stunning demonstration horse. I used Bolt, along with Rock, when I first began to do leadership courses for people in the corporate and sports worlds.

Bolt could be quite a frustrating horse, though, when he started getting into jumping and shows. I knew he could jump anything—I was sure he could jump over a roof—but he had those confidence issues. So one day he'd be able to jump over the roof and the next day he'd slam on his inner brakes and refuse. Everything came down to confidence.

I loved the mental challenge of thinking, 'Right, I've got a week to turn him around,' and trying to figure out why he refused. I'd ask, 'Is his body sore? Is something hurting him?' and if that wasn't it, I had to try to get into his head to understand his attitude. It's what I enjoy most about working with horses—trying to understand why they're making the choices they're making, building those relationships and fine tuning their attitudes until they are 100 per cent focused and keen to please. Trying to find the reason *why* they do something is what it's all about for me.

It's what I enjoy most about working with horses—trying to understand why they're making the choices they're making, building those relationships and fine tuning their attitudes until they are 100 per cent focused and keen to please.

In those first years back in New Zealand I worked long hours, getting inside those horses' heads and learning about their mental landscape, which is just as important as the physical when it comes to getting the very best out of a horse. Everything is about how to build relationships, one horse at a time, horse after horse, from daylight to dusk, working with every different type of horse in every different field until they are the best they can possibly be.

Bolt and I doing loose work (that is, off lead) in the arena.

Rock and I putting on a demonstration for 200 people on the Wellington
waterfront for the Chamber of Commerce Business After 5.

A group of wild horses on Mt Nicholas Station, Queenstown, wondering
when it will be their turn in the yard.

Chance and I showing off our stuff to the Queenstown Chamber of Commerce. Chance went from running twenty lengths behind the last horse to winning by two lengths only five weeks after we first met.

Brave, the one who got away from me on Mt Nicholas Station, settling into life in Wellington before going on to become a top competition horse.

A photo shoot with Bolt, who went from probably the best bucking horse I have ever seen to a great competition and demonstration horse.

Bag work with Maverick on Mt Nicholas Station. The idea is to use the plastic bag as an extension of my arm so I can touch and desensitise a wild horse's body. Maverick was not overly keen to start with, but one year later he was a super-quiet horse that beginners could ride.

With my boy Luca, my best mate, at a cousin's wedding. Luca had the very important job of being the ring bearer.

My little baby girl Tilly (Matilda), who has just turned one.
She is all go-go-go, this one.

The blended family, who get on so well, in Arrowtown. There's a lot of noise when they all get together. From the top: Gwynie Fisk, 10; Allie Fisk, 8; Luca Froggatt, 7; and Tilly Froggatt, 1.

With my gorgeous partner, Sam, and our baby, Tilly, out for dinner in Arrowtown for our third anniversary.

Another shot of my old mate, Rock, and me, about to demonstrate to about 200 business people for the Wellington Chamber of Commerce Business After 5.

'Show me again!'

JUNGLE TALK

Jungle Talk had speed behind him. A racehorse who had been 'galloping the house down' at the training track in Masterton when no one was around, he was a beautiful bay, with a white stripe down his face and three white stockings. He had been in training for about a year and everyone knew he was fast, but his trainer couldn't get him into the trials, much less a race, because they couldn't get him into the starting gates. When they tried, he reared up, jumped out of the stalls and galloped round the track. They tried all sorts of things, but nothing worked. Needless to say, the owner of a fast horse who can't get his horse into the gates is the owner of a horse who is going nowhere fast. His frustrated trainer called me, hoping I would be able to help.

Racehorses are like top athletes. They know that to win they will experience some form of pain—like us, they feel the muscle burn—and if they want to win they have to push through the pain to something else. It's that something else, the mindset of the horse, that is the difference between winning and losing. Some push on through the pain and others give up.

Jungle Talk was the kind of horse who could go the distance. His owner, John Griffin, a retired stock agent, understood it would be possible to help him overcome his fear of the gates, and he was willing to invest in it. It was a challenging scenario in terms of logistics, as even though I had a beautiful environment for him with a 700-metre track, rolling paddocks and the beach just down the road, we didn't have a set of starting gates. So I would have to take Jungle Talk to Levin to work with him there at the gates and then down to the track in Otaki to run. John and I both believed we could get Jungle Talk to a point we knew he had the ability to be. I was looking forward to feeding him up in the paddock with hay and giving him some mates for company.

I liked Jungle Talk as soon as I saw him. He was an athlete with a kind face and eye, and it was clear he was a horse who really used his brain. As with all the horses I work with, the first thing I wanted to do was get a good look at the state of him and his physical condition. I want to get the horses happy in their environment. With Jungle, I rugged him up and fed him well and put him out on a little bit of grass. I always make a mental note of all the things that might need to be done to get the horse up to scratch and looking a million dollars, including its feet, teeth and body, and if necessary I bring in people like chiropractors and massage therapists.

I liked Jungle Talk as soon as I saw him. He was an athlete with a kind face and eye, and it was clear he was a horse who really used his brain.

Jungle was a horse who had no respect for people. In a way it wasn't his fault, as he had never really been told how to behave otherwise. So the first thing we did was a series of lessons designed to set up some personal space. Because of the focus on improving his gate work, I needed him to have a lot of respect because we would be working in tight spaces together in the gates. Then we worked his hindquarters.

I consider it disrespectful if horses turn their hindquarters to me. I work on that and then move on to walking into the horse's space and getting the horse to back away from me. Just like with the wild horses, these are ways of setting up boundaries and respect. Then I do some activities where I stand still and feed out some energy and get the horses to back away. All the time I'm building a relationship with them.

As I'm assessing any horse, I ask myself these essential questions along the way: Are they trying? Are they avoiding?

Are they focused? Are they trying to get out of this? I am looking at how they react to the little things. With Jungle it was clear he had an athlete's attitude and learned very quickly.

When we are lunging and engaging in transitions I'm trying to get the horse to trot and move into different paces to see how well it is listening and how quickly it responds. Jungle did a lot of hand walking for an hour every day. This is where a horse is walked on a lead rope as opposed to being ridden. I like hand walking because walking is the pace where they use every muscle in their body. There's no stress or strain on the body. It's a way to build some light muscle on a skinny, scrawny horse while it's gaining some weight.

Jungle loved to run, he was a keen-to-learn, go-go-go kind of horse. We used to joke that he pulled like a train, but as he was a real athlete with a beautiful temperament, he just wanted to go. Still, the first time I took him to the gates I could tell he was really worried.

When Jungle first came to me I said to his trainer, 'So you've spent a bit of time with him in the gates?'

'Yup, yup.'

'How much time?'

'About five minutes.'

Needless to say, when Jungle got in there he was pretty unhappy, so he figured he'd just smash his way out. The next time he was taken to the gates he was again worried about what was going to happen, so the trainer got him in under sedation. Now Jungle developed a huge worry.

He was afraid of the gates and what had happened in there. So every time he saw the gates he just filled up with worry. Because Jungle was a thinker, he started to use his brain, but his thoughts just convinced him all the more that the way to stay safe was to stay away from those gates.

I'm really patient, especially when I'm working with a horse like Jungle. I guess it comes from two things. The first is I'm confident the horse can do what is asked of it—it's just a question of time. The second is I want my horses to be comfortable doing something because they have done it many times, under many different circumstances, so when it comes to race day it's just like any other day.

As a result, I am thorough in every aspect of what we do. I'll tell the horse, 'I don't believe you. Show me again, show me again, show me again.' Every day is another day. I like to see five or six days where a negative habit is no longer showing up before I'm sure. Every day is different, and I want to make sure the bad habit has gone. We also don't move onto the next stage until I feel really confident about the last one. Otherwise we're just building on poor foundations, and there's nothing to be gained from it.

In Jungle Talk's case, I was confident that, even if he raced through those gates four days in a row, eventually he would slow down and get it right. I knew he had a lot of worry, but eventually we were going to wear it down through repetition and practice. Most people doubt themselves, but I don't. Worrying about the outcome would have been a waste of time, because on day five Jungle Talk was finally ready and he just went right on through those gates at a walk.

I learned, too, because we were spending so much time loading him in and out of the horse truck, to take him to Levin and Otaki, that his issue wasn't about a fear of tight places. It was about the gates themselves. He never minded getting in and out of the truck.

I put him on a long rope and had him stand a metre off the gates. As the gates opened, I would step to the side as he flew past me. In the first few days there were plenty of close calls where I felt the wind rush past as he blew by me. We did this more than a hundred times in the first few days with little change. And just as he was making progress, it was heartbreaking that he might smack against the gates again, which would set him back. He would lose confidence and we'd go back to the beginning. But the important part was we just kept trying. I never lost any hope he would get there.

I varied my approach with him, too, as horses need time off and time to process. This is often hard when we feel we are working to a time frame, but I always try to do what's best for the horse. Giving the horse processing time will save time in the long run. It's the art of knowing when to apply pressure and when to take it off. Just like kids at school, drilling horses until they are thoroughly sick of something doesn't necessarily make things better. At school I can't remember liking any subject that was endlessly drilled.

I once read something Bart Cummings, master trainer of twelve Melbourne Cup winners, said he did. A few days after a big race, he would take his horses for a little stroll then stand and watch them have a pick of grass.

He stood there quietly, just watching and listening. He was waiting to see if the horse would tell him whether it was ready to run again soon, or if it needed more time. By spending just a little bit of time reading the horses and listening to what they said, he could gauge where they were at.

With Jungle Talk, each of our sessions started out with us just walking, Jungle poodling along, now and then stopping to pick some grass as he went. In that time, too, he was starting to figure out I was different from other humans he had met. For one thing, I wasn't going away, and though he could try some of the tricks that had worked well for him in the past, in the end he and I both knew he was going to walk through those gates. He was learning, too, that I am kind and fair, and that there would be lots of praise when he got it right. I was doing everything I could to treat him like Kiwi, giving him an environment where he could be happy and flourish. And he was learning to trust me and grow in confidence.

At the gates, we practised with lots of noise all around. This idea is similar to 'bagging', where I want to desensitise the horse. I would stand up alongside the gates and bang and bang them. On race day, while Jungle Talk might be calm and fine with the gates, I couldn't guarantee the horse next to him wouldn't be crashing around and making a racket. I wanted him to be calm and ready to run in any circumstances, like an athlete being 'in the zone'. The last thing I wanted was for him to be feeling really good on race day then to have another horse setting him off.

I wanted to make sure he didn't feel trapped, so we did a lot of practice with the gates wide open: if he wasn't happy he could back out and then come in again. I would stand up there and swing the gates from side to side, and he would look at me, saying, 'I'm cool with that. Everything's fine.' I needed to make sure I had tried everything so I could send him out, confident he would be better at the gates than any of the other horses.

On race day, while Jungle Talk might be calm and fine with the gates, I couldn't guarantee the horse next to him wouldn't be crashing around and making a racket.

After that I moved from practising with the gates open to closing them. Again, at every stage I was reading him, checking to see if his head was low and relaxed. I stayed above him, rubbing him, too, as I wanted him to get accustomed to the idea I was there for him. Later, when the pressure was on, I wanted him to feel he could look up if he needed to and say to himself, 'Andrew's there. It's all good.' And even if I couldn't be there, a gate attendant could be.

For a horse like Jungle Talk who'd had some bad experiences in the past, part of what I do is replace these with good experiences. Horses thank us for releasing all their baggage and tension. If horses have been on the receiving end of other people's lack of knowledge, my hope is that when I've worked with them, even if their owner continues to make some average decisions, at least the horses will know right from wrong. They will have manners, and effectively know how to say please and thank you. I'm giving them the skills so they know what to do, and hopefully it will keep them out of trouble in the future when I'm not around. If they've had a good education and it's been instilled well, they'll know the right thing to do in most situations and become thinking horses.

Five weeks into our time together we took Jungle to the jumpouts, which is a training race of about six to eight horses, and he won by six lengths. Ten days later we took him to the thoroughbred racing trials at Waverley, where only the officials were allowed to touch him. The pressure was on, the tension was high, and I was asking myself if I had left any stone unturned. As he walked in, I can still hear the announcer saying, 'Jungle Talk stands well.' The gates opened, Jungle was out first, led all the way, turned into the straight, put his foot down and won by five lengths with his ears pricked, which meant he did it all pretty easily.

I was thrilled. Over lunch John told me he had just been offered some big money, $200,000, for Jungle Talk, but he wasn't for sale. After lunch, I met the trainer in the tie-up stalls, we shook hands, and he loaded Jungle onto the truck to take him back to Masterton. My job was done.

I was sad to see Jungle leave, and I missed him as soon as he walked up into the truck. We had spent a lot of time together and I marvelled at how far he had come from when we first met. I would have loved to have taken him home and spoiled him after he had performed so well, but it was time for him to go back to the trainer. He had his own life to lead. That's one of the quiet but difficult parts of this kind of work. Sometimes it's hard to say goodbye.

I would have loved to have taken him home and spoiled him . . . but he had his own life to lead.

EARLIER I MENTIONED THAT the first thing I did when Jungle Talk arrived was to take a good look at him and assess his condition. This is something I always do. Before I start to work with a horse I need to work out if there is a particular reason for the way it's behaving—is the horse trying to say it's in pain? Is something bothering it, or is it more an issue of education and attitude?

If a horse is communicating it is really unhappy or something is hurting, it's important for us to notice and act. So the first thing I do is make sure the horse isn't suffering physically. I begin at the ground and work my way up. First I bring in a farrier to have a look at its feet. Horses have amazingly sensitive feet, and they can suffer from a variety of foot-related problems. The ground they stand on can really affect their feet, and sometimes what they are eating can also influence their foot health. For instance, thoroughbreds, who have a lot of grain in their feed, often have bad feet. If you have a horse with bad feet, one thing you can do is take it off the grain and put it on good grass. It often helps really quickly.

If you have a horse with bad feet, one thing you can do is take it off the grain and put it on good grass.

From the feet I move up to the horse's back and bring in either a horse massage therapist or a chiropractor. In many cases the problem lies in the back. The horse can be in great pain and we don't know it, but every time we put a saddle on a horse who's suffering back problems, well, you can imagine how it would feel. No wonder it wants to throw you off!

In my experience, 90 per cent of bucking horses are either sore or suffering from a saddle that doesn't fit. For instance, if a younger horse who has been good with the saddle and has had quite a bit of riding suddenly starts to turn around and nip when it is being saddled, to me it's a sign it's starting to feel a bit tight around the girth. This is the type of situation where it's important to both notice and act, not ignore it. Over the years some of my most frustrating clients have been those who've been told their horse is sore, and I've referred them to someone who could help, but when I see them several weeks later nothing has changed. If they needed a massage themselves, they'd get one, so it's frustrating when they won't do the same for their horses.

On the other hand, I've also seen the opposite—those owners who do care a great deal and want to help their horses, even horses who may have caused them great harm. I once worked with a man who had bought himself a thoroughbred horse to ride on the weekends when he and his wife were out at their property in the Wairarapa. The first time he climbed on this horse, it bucked him off, throwing him so hard he broke his neck and three vertebrae. He was in a brace for over six weeks while he recovered.

He sent the horse to me. I ran him through my system and couldn't find much wrong. The horse was quiet and had a good attitude, but because it was a thoroughbred and was only getting fed on the weekends, it probably wasn't the ideal breed for what the owner wanted. While I was waiting for a massage therapist to come and see him, I fed him up, as he had seemed a little light. After a while, we got him to the point where he was willing to tolerate a rider, and we made sure he had quite a few massages. Eventually we had the vet look at him.

We found that a couple of bones in his back were starting to fuse together. Sometimes they were all right, but at other times, if he'd done something in the paddock, or the saddle sat on him in an uncomfortable way, he would be in uncontrollable pain and had to get the rider off him as quickly as he could.

In the end we all discussed the situation, especially as it related to safety, and even though he was a beautiful thoroughbred he just ended up being a paddock mate for other horses and couldn't be ridden. I've always appreciated that story because it reminds us all we need to think from the horse's perspective. He wasn't a naughty horse. He was bucking for a reason, and the reason was he was in a lot of pain!

It also really helped that the owner could see things from the horse's point of view, even if he had landed him with a broken back. Previously the horse had had a really hard life and been abused, but this owner just wanted to treat him with kindness.

If I've looked at a horse's feet and its back and it's still having problems, I'll also give its mouth a good look. Horse's teeth are different to those of many other animals. They keep growing continuously throughout their lives, so horses have to grind their teeth down through grazing and eating or they can experience serious problems. If a horse is having riding and steering problems, these often indicate issues in its mouth, and that's why they're struggling with the bit.

One of the overall indicators of a horse's health is whether it is skinny or looking well fed. Is it looking run down, with skin issues? There are a lot of people who let their horses get really skinny. They'll say, 'Well, it's winter,' as if they expect their horse to get really skinny in winter. I always ask them, 'Do you get skinny in winter? You still feed yourself!' Often, people just aren't really taking responsibility for their horse, and it's become skinny because it's hardly been fed. The issue of weight tells me as much about the person looking after the horse as it does about the horse itself.

If pain has been ruled out as the source of a horse's behaviour, then I ask what else could be the cause. Does it have a specific fear? Is it remembering a traumatic experience and reliving it every time it gets into the same circumstances, like Jungle Talk in the gates? Has it been abused in the past in such a way it has never learned to trust people?

The more I work with a horse, the more I'm interested in what is 'normal' for that horse both in terms of pain tolerance and then more broadly in terms of behaviour. If you've ever been in hospital for something pain related, you might have been asked, 'On a scale of one to ten, what's your pain like today?' It can be useful in determining how much pain you feel you're experiencing. But it also helps if they know you, too, as it may be you're a person of extremes and your pain is always going to be described as a ten even if it's actually a two. It seems it's the same with horses. From the beginning I'm looking to see if a horse has a high pain tolerance and is a sort of Richie McCaw of horses, able to play a championship game on a broken foot, or if it is a highly strung diva horse who feels the weight of a fly on its flanks as if it were a hundredweight.

Learning to read the pain-to-drama ratio in a horse is critical for a couple of reasons. In a horse who has a high pain tolerance and a low expression of drama, it might not know something is really bothering it until it has pushed itself too far. Equally, if I know a horse is very pain oriented and has a high level of sensitivity, I can begin to gauge what is real, what is imagined, and where the horse can be encouraged to get a grip on itself.

When is that important?

Well, you might have a horse who has a really low pain tolerance. In that case, as a safety measure you might want to let only experienced riders on it because if the horse felt a twinge of something its first reaction could be to buck you off. On the other hand, what if you had a horse who you knew had a really high pain tolerance? Then, if it showed signs of something wrong you'd know to get it checked out straight away, because it wasn't normally a horse who made a fuss, so it must be in serious pain. If these horses were people, one might be the hypochondriac, convinced he's dying when he's got a head cold, and the other one is granddad on his deathbed, telling the doctor not to fuss over him because it's not so bad.

If these horses were people, one might be the hypochondriac, convinced he's dying when he's got a head cold, and the other one is granddad on his deathbed, telling the doctor not to fuss over him because it's not so bad.

I try to work with the farrier, the chiropractor and the veterinarians to figure out what is pain related or soreness for the horse, and what is attitude. The two are naturally tied together because if the horse is holding a lot of tension, it will amplify any soreness. On the other hand, if the medical team is able to release the soreness, this can release the tension, and then the horse stands a much better chance of being open to learning because it has the energy for it.

If I know a horse's issues are about attitude, well, that's when I know we can make huge progress, because there is no horse who doesn't want to learn something new. Some are tough. Some take longer than others. Some are real problems and they can take a lot more time. If I was going to buy a horse, I'd buy a really beautiful, talented problem horse, because they've seen the bad side of people already. When I get them into my environment, they'll do absolutely anything for me. What I like about those horses, too, is that they're usually the good ones because they're tough and smart. They have got the better of humans thus far, but I know I can turn them around and get them working for me as opposed to against me. I know I can get the best out of them. When the going gets tough in a race or competition they can climb through the pain barrier, just like a human athlete, and keep going where the others give in.

But to get there, every horse—regardless of whether it is beautiful, tough, dramatic, stubborn, or all of the above at the same time—goes along the same training path. And this ultimately has everything to do with creating safety, for me, for anyone who interacts with the horse, and for the horse itself.

Safety is important for many reasons. I remember when I was ten and I got my first horse, Bobby. I didn't know anything. That experience made me very conscious of how it feels not to know what you're doing around a horse. Bobby was pretty keen to get the best of me, and for a while he did. I've always known that if you don't feel safe with a horse your energy isn't going to be good, and how can you work well with a horse if you're just conveying you're afraid? The horse is going to walk all over you. Sometimes literally.

But also, and maybe more importantly, horses need to be animals who are safe to be around. They need to know the 'right behaviour' for interacting with people. They may have a set of behaviours they use to keep themselves in check when they're in their own bands, but in our world they need 'good manners' and to know that kicking, biting, bucking and rearing are not remotely appropriate. I want to know that my kids, or anyone's kids, can be safe walking around the back of any horse I'm working with, and that the horse would never think to kick them. I have to be that sure.

My goals when working with horses, as with people, are pretty simple:

- Create the right environment to bring out the best.
- Create clear boundaries.
- Build a trusting relationship.
- Establish clear lines of communication.
- Reinforce consistency.
- Build confidence in the horse.
- Develop a keenness to please in the horse.

I believe in the potential of every horse to perform to the best of its abilities, and because of that, horses trust me. What I guess I don't always believe in as much as I believe in a horse's willingness to change is people's willingness to change. At the end of the day, horses reflect back to us our actions and choices, not the words we say or what we claim our intentions are. This is what makes them such a good teaching tool for us.

Horses are exceptional mirrors of all the principles that matter so much in how we interact with anyone in a relationship. They show us the rewards of our patience and willingness to take the time necessary for real learning to take place, the rewards of stability that come from clarity of communication and consistency, and the potential to achieve creative success or 'personal best' if a horse, or a person, is believed in and given all the best tools.

Horses reflect back to us our actions and choices, not the words we say or what we claim our intentions are. This is what makes them such a good teaching tool for us.

So given all that, which doesn't sound too hard, it's sad so many relationships between horses and people end up being less than ideal. I've come to believe that where knowledge ends, violence starts, and the less people know of how to treat a horse well, or to get inside its head, the more frustration there will be, and the more pain. The corollary of this is that the more knowledge people have, and the more effort they make to really understand their horse, the more rewarding their relationship will be.

I've been particularly lucky to have had a few great human teachers, and some truly outstanding ones on four legs. If nothing else, they've taught me to keep my wits about me, but probably more importantly, to have a good sense of humour.

Building a relationship

ROCK

My partner, Sam, jokes that, for a guy who spends his time working with horses, I talk a lot about relationships. A couple of times she's told me I might be better at woman whispering if I wasn't paying so much attention to horse whispering, but I know she's teasing (or I hope she is!). Truth is, I do spend a lot of time thinking about relationships, because it doesn't matter whether you're working with a horse or paying attention to your kids, the fundamentals are the same. And there's no better way to see how horses can mirror back to us how we are—rather than what we say—than in our relationships with them.

Outside my relationship with my family, my longest and most enduring relationship is with a chestnut pony. These days I think of him as my 'old guy', but really he's still more like my partner in crime. Rock's his name, and if ever someone's name fitted their character, it'd be this guy. Apart from a two-year break, we've been together for over twenty years. It's a bit like an old marriage now. We sure have had enough battles of will. I always win in the end, and Rock knows it, but what I like best about him is that he's always made me work for it.

You wouldn't know it now if you looked at him, but back in the day Rock had attitude, a kind of X factor that came more from who he thought he was than what he actually looked like. If he'd been a person, he would have turned heads on attitude alone. He was also very, very smart.

Rock and his brother Pamper were both bred by an old fella from Greytown, in the Wairarapa, a friend of my grandfather's who ran a printing business. He said he named them after two Greek wind gods, Pamperos and Roceros, but those are pretty hard names to wrap your mouth around, so by the time I got to know them they had paddock names—Pamper and Rock. The old guy had bred the horses for his grandchildren but none of the kids wanted them, so although they had been broken in they had been more or less left on their own.

Rock and Pamper came to me in 1993, when I was just back from Melbourne and keen to work with some horses of my own. Rock already had a reputation for being something of a show-off who always wanted to be in on the action.

He had been kept down in the Marlborough Sounds where the old fellow had a bach. Then he had been broken in by a woman from the South Island who really liked him, and one time she asked if she could take him on a three-day lamb muster, riding her own horse and leading Rock. Instead, Rock orchestrated things so she rode him and led her horse. The old fellow told me that sometimes he would take another horse down to the beach and leave Rock in the paddock, only to find Rock following along behind on his own a couple of minutes later. That's what I loved about him—he would just jump out of a situation if he didn't want to be there.

I remember the first time I saw Rock I felt really disappointed, as he wasn't what I was expecting. I had spoken to the old guy a couple of times on the phone and he had been raving about Rock. It had taken him all his life to breed such a beautiful big horse, he said. He kept going on about how big Rock was, so I suppose in my mind I was picturing a big 17-hand horse.

He was put on an open-sided barge and sailed across to Picton, then loaded onto a horse truck and taken on the ferry to Wellington. I went down to the waterfront to pick him up, looking forward to seeing this big horse, and out of the truck strutted this little 15.1 (15 hands, 1 inch tall, i.e. 60 inches) chestnut horse who looked more like a pony than a horse. But I thought, let's get him home, settle him in, get to know him and then see what he's like.

Rock was like a fox terrier of a horse. Cocky, arrogant, 'I'm the man, I'm the best.' To me, once I got to know him, he was Christmas. But with his attitude, it wasn't surprising we had a few battles. One day I caught him and we needed to cross a bit of bog. I learned then that Rock didn't like getting his feet wet, so he just wasn't going to have it. He met me with a big 'No way, Andrew,' and I met him with an 'Oh yes, Rock.' There was definitely a battle of wills going on. I had thought walking across that stretch of bog was going to save us twenty minutes, but it ended up being two hours of a really good lesson for us both, and yes, in the end I won.

Rock was like a fox terrier of a horse. Cocky, arrogant, 'I'm the man, I'm the best.'

Rock was as tough and as strong-willed as I was, but he was also very smart. He could be totally unreasonable and just say, 'No, sorry, not doing it,' and he had the toughness to go on and on about not doing it. On the whole he was really quiet, but he could have been a real problem horse for a lot of people because he was just so smart. And he was such an arrogant bugger in the paddock with the other horses, too. He didn't limit himself to humans on that front. Other horses didn't always like him. Horses will follow the leader who gets them out of situations, not the one who gets them into situations. Just like people, horses don't really like a cocky youngster too much.

Our relationship has certainly had its ups and downs. But in the end, it's been a bit like making a marriage work. Putting in the time. Showing up for each other. Consistency. Laughter. Understanding each other and being there in the good times and the hard times. Worrying about the other one's happiness and trying to do your best to make them happy. Over the years Rock and I have demonstrated to thousands of people, and he has been a huge part of getting me to where I am today. He has also taken me from nervously addressing a crowd to being able to speak confidently in front of two or three hundred people. When Rock is by my side, everything is easy.

He has also been a vital partner in getting out and promoting our corporate leadership courses. When people saw our demonstrations, they understood what I was trying to teach. Just as he once deceived me with his size, people would start off seeing a quiet little chestnut pony, until I turned on the switch and he exploded, off lead, into the quickest thing on four legs, stopping centimetres from my face.

Rock is now retired, and I do all I can to give him the best possible life and make sure he is happy. I dread the day when I find him in the paddock or have to make that hard decision, but I will always put what is best for him ahead of my own feelings. I know when the day comes it will affect me more than even the people closest to me will understand. I love that horse and all he has done for me.

SO THAT'S THE STORY of my lifelong companion, but how do you start out on that relationship with a new horse? I've worked with thousands of horses in my career, and while there has only been one Rock for me, I've had great relationships with many other horses, too.

What makes what I do different from many people is that I am very thorough at every single step. I don't move forward until I'm sure every stage is ingrained and fully understood by the horse. I start off the same way with every horse, regardless of what it is going to go on to do. There are six first steps, a programme of readiness, and everything else follows from there. For the horse it's like learning good manners, but at the same time it's teaching me things about the horse so we can build the best possible relationship. The foundations of every relationship are really exactly the same.

I always begin with safety. A relationship is only as good and only as deep as it is safe, both on the emotional plane and on the physical. How do I create safety? Through the use of six stages of groundwork, just as I did with those wild horses at Mt Nicholas all those years ago. These stages are designed to set up some basic boundaries, make the horse more responsive, get control of the hindquarters, gain control of their feet, and to start to make the horse supple on both sides. Along with working on the horse's physical side, I also work on its mental state and tweaking its attitude so it is really keen to please. As we go through the steps I am discovering aspects of the horse's attitude, whether or not it is quiet, or if it is going to be one of my time bombs waiting to explode.

At the base of this system is how the horses learn, which is through the application and release of pressure. I also use a clicking sound a lot with horses (and sometimes with my family, especially my lovely partner, Sam, who occasionally hears me do it unconsciously when she's running late). Clicking is my way of saying, 'Come on, hurry up!' Clicking is the lightest form of pressure, so I always start with this. Then I slowly start to build up some energy to move the horse, using more and more until it does what I am asking, then I stop and praise it to communicate it has done the right thing. If I use my energy to motivate and move the horse I can use less pressure, meaning I am being softer and lighter.

If I use my energy to motivate and move the horse I can use less pressure, meaning I am being softer and lighter.

I think about the six steps I take with the horses as being like a pilot's pre-flight check. The last thing you want is to be at 35,000 feet and discover the plane's engines aren't going to be able to take you where you want to go. It's similar with a horse. I want to know the horse's potential capabilities, what might be pent up inside it that hasn't been released, and where we're likely to have to spend more time. I often find out from the horse what it knows or doesn't know by how it reacts. I want to know that by the time we've finished working through these initial stages the horse will be safe for me, and other people, to work with. At the end of the day, everything comes down to safety.

What I am trying to do is build a relationship with the horse where we both want the best outcomes. In the end, the horse will do anything I ask of it, not because I've asked, but because it wants to do those things. That's the real goal, to motivate that horse, making my ideas its ideas. I care about the mental readiness of the horse as much as I care about its physical readiness. In fact, I probably care about its head space even more. In working with the so-called worst of the worst problem horses over the last twenty years, the way in which I can take an animal who seems like a wound-up nutcase, full of tension, and turn it into a horse who is calm, consistent and reliable has everything to do with getting it to start to use its brain. It's taking the horse from a first response of 'run, panic, flee' to instead 'stop, look and think'. Just like a person, when a horse actually stops and thinks, things are never as bad as they seem.

In the first stage, I establish a boundary. I want to create a safe distance between the horse and myself. I like this to be about an arm's length, which just establishes some personal space. Boundaries are essential in life, and horses need to know where my space is. This is also my first opportunity to convey what I mean by consistency to the horse. We're going to know each other at an arm's length. If the horse enters my space, I'm not going to take a step back, because that's going to tell the horse it's the leader here. Instead, I'm going to stand my ground, not with any drama, but simply making it clear this is the appropriate distance we keep, and taking it back to where it should be.

To do this, I call the horse towards me and then put my arm out to stop it at arm's length. If the horse continues to come, I hold my ground, and let the horse walk into my hand. I'm laidback, but I mean what I say. Then the horse says, 'Wow, you mean it,' and I say, 'Yes, I do.' I can't be any nicer than that, but when I say something I mean it. Often during our courses I see people saying they want the horse to stop, but their body language says the opposite. They are leaning backwards instead of forwards, and not projecting confidence to the horse—indicating they don't really mean it. The horse knows they don't mean what they say. While it rarely actually happens, the idea that the horse 'walked all over you' is pretty much what's happening.

Often during our courses I see people saying they want the horse to stop, but their body language says the opposite. They are leaning backwards instead of forwards, and not projecting confidence to the horse—indicating they don't really mean it.

One of the challenges horses face in trying to read what we want from them is that many of us send out mixed messages. Horses are endlessly trying to figure us out. They generally want to please, and they want to understand what the codes of good engagement with us are. The problem is, if we're not consistent in how we interact with them or don't show them what our expectations for our relationship are, the horse is left guessing. It might be picking up patterns in our behaviour we are not even aware of. That's why they are such accurate reflectors of our actual behaviour, not what we say we want to be or do.

With most horses it doesn't take too long to establish this basic boundary. The key is not so much creating the boundary as being consistent in maintaining it. I can't just say to the horse that sometimes it's OK to be at this distance and sometimes it's not: every time we're together, it will just spend its time testing that boundary, and it is likely to be really confused. I am always reinforcing and correcting this basic boundary. It's important that all the little things, the basics, are going well, which means bigger issues don't have a chance to develop.

Once the horse knows it can't step into my space, in the next task I am going to establish myself as the boss of the relationship. I am going to be a nice, kind, fair boss. I'm going to say that if the horse respects me, I can move into its space and it is going to get out of my way. Often, at the races or a show, it's common to see horses dragging people around and sometimes even two people leading a horse, with one on either side. As far as I'm concerned, that horse has no respect for them. Sometimes the horses are hardly even noticing the people around them. They are just off on their own agenda. But things don't have to be like that, and we are making even the most basic of tasks like leading a horse all the more difficult if we let this happen. If the horses had respect for people, they wouldn't act like this.

On the subject of respect, there's the old way of doing things, which is 'You do this or some form of pain is coming your way,' or we can build a relationship and get the respect in this way. Over the years, in racing circles, I have often seen good horses being allowed to get away with murder, biting and carrying on like spoiled brats. This is based on the idea that the trainer doesn't want to break the horse's spirit, which of course I support. That's the last thing I would want to do. But the other thing is they just don't know what to do about it. We all know we need to put some boundaries in place to stop bad behaviour, and most of the time, animals are behaving this way because they aren't happy. We can still say, 'No, this isn't acceptable,' without being too harsh or breaking the horse's spirit, but it does need to know we are the boss, and when we say 'Don't' or 'No', we mean it.

So again, what I do is create some personal space and set it up as a big 'no-no' for the horse to come into my space and push me around. If I am consistent with this, the horse can never get into my space to bite or push. The next thing is I want to be able to walk into the horse's space and, if it respects me, it will get out of my way. The way I do this is with energy. Remember the story of Loco who jumped out of the pen just because I had stepped closer to her? She was an example of the way in which horses feel energy.

With domesticated horses, things are not usually quite so extreme. Just the lightest form of pressure is needed. What

I will do is walk towards the horse with a little bit of intent, carrying myself like I really expect the horse to move and get out of the way. Horses are our best teachers here, and if they don't feel the energy, they won't move.

Our energy and how we use it is really important. We want to be nice and relaxed, as that's how we want our horses to be, but we have to have a bit of presence that says, 'Hey, I mean you to do this now.' Too much energy and the horse will overreact, too little and it won't move at all, so we need to find the balance. I always break this down, first taking one step, then two, and so on. As the horse starts to get the idea, the next stage is to pick up the speed a little, so when I ask them something they start responding with more urgency. For a horse who is used to walking all over people or dragging them around, teaching them to be really respectful around these basic boundaries will make them a lot more thoughtful and attentive to what we are doing around them.

The next thing I do is move the hindquarters, as this is where all the horse's power is. All of my horses are taught that if I come towards them, they should just stand still. But if I go wider around them, they are to move their back end and turn and face me. Imagine opening a stable door. You don't want to meet the horse's back end. You want it moved, and for the horse to turn and face you, as much for good manners as for safety.

A few years back I did a trip to Hong Kong which involved three days of meetings with some big companies. I was selling my corporate leadership courses, and also spent four days teaching and giving lessons at a riding school which had

45 horses on just over a hectare of land. These poor horses had never seen a paddock. There was nowhere for them to go, and the instructors were not allowed to hack them out, so the horses' lives were spent going from the stable to the arena. I learned if they couldn't earn their keep doing two or three riding lessons a day they couldn't stay. It made me realise just how lucky our New Zealand horses are.

You don't want to meet the horse's back end. You want it moved, and for the horse to turn and face you, as much for good manners as for safety.

Their team consisted of six full-time English riding instructors and fourteen Pakistani workers who were in charge of mucking out the stables and keeping the place tidy. On the final afternoon of my visit, I was asked to show the staff how to go about entering the boxes for the afternoon muck-out and feeding. Nine of the horses were getting really aggressive and had been biting when they were disturbed in the afternoons. Naturally, all the staff had become pretty scared of having to go in with them. The result was the staff weren't able to do things properly, and the horses had suffered.

I went from box to box, catching the horses and speaking in a soft voice. As I came into the boxes, the horses would pin their ears back with nasty-looking faces and start to lunge at me. It was pretty scary stuff in a small space with nowhere to go, not to mention an audience of about twenty people standing outside! I figured all these horses were just trying to intimidate me, so I kept talking gently and put my hand out, saying, 'I just want to come in and give you a rub.' They stopped in front of me, looking confused because I hadn't turned and bolted like the staff had. I then just carried on and rubbed them. They were still pulling faces but now I was relaxed and ready to move if I had to; I just kept rubbing and talking and moving on in. From the horses' point of view, although they were still pulling faces, I just went on in and did what I wanted. As they saw that what they were doing wasn't working, they were smart enough to try something different.

Some of the horses also turned their back ends towards me, so I gave them a flick with the rope, pushed them away then backed them off so they had room to turn and face me. Then I set it up so I moved around the side of the box with the horse in the middle, to teach them that everywhere I went, they would have to turn and face me, or they would get pushed away. In setting up these basics, teaching them always to look at me, and making a fuss of them when they did, I could start to break those habits that were developing.

Now, I still had fourteen staff who needed to learn how to do this themselves. I told them the biggest thing they had to do was talk, because nervous and tense people can start to hold their breath and the horses pick up their fear and play on it. They also had to learn to try and project confidence to the horse, even if they were scared. In the end, it all worked out well. For the staff, it felt like they were putting their lives in my hands, but they trusted me, and when they came out of the stable they were hugely relieved and smiling. Afterwards, I spent time with the owner, suggesting a variety of different things she could do to mix it up for the horses and try to make them happier.

ONCE THE HORSES ARE good at moving their hindquarters, the next thing I do is some more backing up. This time, I stand still and feed out energy to back the horses to the end of my rope. Once again I break this down into a couple of steps back, then I give the horse a rub, then go for a few more steps, always breaking it into easy chunks for the horse to understand.

From here we move on to lunging. This is where I get the horses moving around me, doing transitions, which basically means varying the speed from walk to trot to canter. It allows me to gauge how well the horse is listening by how quickly they respond. I often tell people who are lunging horses to think of the shoulder on the horse being the balance point. If we are in front, the horse will go backwards, and if we are behind, we can drive the horse forward. I always start in front of the horse, making it clear with an outstretched hand which direction I want it to go, and then I aim some pressure just behind the shoulder to move the horse out and get it going forward. Forwardness is one of the main things I'm looking for, developing nice paces, and working at getting the horse suppling around the corners.

After lunging, I want to work on isolating particular parts of the horse's body, the idea being that we want to get control of the mind and the feet. Once I start to do this I am gaining some pretty good basic control of the horse, speeding it up, slowing it down, and moving it in any direction. First I want to move only the front end of the horse. I do this by asking the horse to keep its hind feet still and only move its front feet in response to the task I've asked of it. Then I do the same thing with the hind end. Again I want to have a horse who is thinking all the time, so as the tasks become increasingly difficult, it is using its mind to figure out how to do it well.

In the last stage, I ask the horse to do side passing, which involves getting it to move across and away from me, a complicated kind of manoeuvre where I start to really see the horse's capacity for doing complex tasks. This is the one the horses themselves probably struggle with the most, and some can feel the pressure, so it's quite good for taking a read on where a particular horse is at.

While all these steps could be seen as mainly physical tasks, they are also enabling me to learn about the horse's mental and emotional strengths. This is the aspect of the training that is probably the hardest to convey except through experience. It is really no different from a teacher working with a class full of students who may have been assigned the same task, where some will rush through it, others will be slow and steady, and some will burst into tears of frustration. It's really about assessing the horse and developing your relationship with it as it increases its capacity for more complex tasks.

In conjunction with these exercises, I also use a lot of reverse psychology. In doing this I often let the horses do what they want to do, but make their ideas harder and harder before again suggesting my idea, which then becomes the easy option for them. Remember Rhythm in the Wind, who backed up half a kilometre because he didn't want to go forward? Or Beanie and the float, where reverse psychology helped convince him that staying in the float was far better than flying out? What I like about this is that the horse makes its own decision to do something; it has tried its way, which is hard, so then it can choose the easy option.

My own self-control is very important in this. Imagine if I have been working with a problem horse for a month and have built up a good relationship, then one day I come out short-tempered and snap? From then on, the horse would always look at me a little differently and I would lose the trust I'd built up. Luckily, I am extremely patient and can quietly work away at something for hours and hours, but for people who are not naturally patient, this approach gives them the confidence they will get the results in the end.

Some of the really tough horses can handle a fair bit of working around—you just have to be confident you are on the right track and will achieve your goal. I think this is where a lot of people go wrong. They doubt whether they are doing the right thing and can give up too easily, but you never know when the horse will soften. It might be in five minutes or an hour, but I know they *will* soften.

An example of where this can be used is around floats. If a horse wants to pull away from the float, make it your idea and back it up further and further. Sometimes I will even turn the horse around and back it up to the float. Again, I'm using reverse psychology by making backing away hard and standing at the float easy.

I work with a lot of horses and their owners, and nothing makes me happier than seeing them move from a place of frustration in their relationship to one where they are both facing the same direction, and can go on and have some fun. When everyone starts to get it right, there are endless opportunities for creating the best relationships in the world. When we create the right environment, where we bring out the best in the horse, have its trust and respect, and its attitude is fine-tuned to one where it is eager to please, there is nothing we can't do with our horses.

The dream

KING GURU

I've probably always been something of a dreamer, or if not a dreamer, a visualiser. I'm also a perfectionist, and I don't seem to be able to rest if I see a job that needs doing and has been left undone. I'm not saying it's necessarily a good trait or a bad one. It just happens that I notice small things and details as much as I visualise the big picture. Sometimes the two go really well together. Sometimes they mean I don't sleep much.

All my life I've carried around a few big dreams. The first one, thanks to Kiwi, was to take a horse to the Melbourne Cup and win it. That's still really high on my list, and there's a good chance I'll get there. The second dream was to find a place where I would be able to offer the leadership courses I've always wanted to do, where horses become teachers for people in the realm of personal and professional development. For a long time I wanted to make this happen, but I didn't want to bring people to a place that wasn't ideal for that kind of learning. In my imagination, I could see how it would be. Post and rail fences. A beautiful arena. Rolling hills and places for people to sit. Barns. Horses—lots and lots of horses. Some of the horses would be re-educated, some would be tamed for the first time, some would be trained for racing, and some would be part of the development courses. It would be perfect.

By the late 1990s I had been working up and down the coast around Wellington for a few years and building up a reputation, especially in the racing industry, as someone who could work with problem horses. Eventually I was able to lease a 16-hectare property up the coast where I could house horses. I had 25 horses on the go and I was working daylight to dusk, but it was a good way to learn how to run a big property like that.

One of the first people I worked with there was a woman who had inherited a thoroughbred she had left in the paddock to become just skin and bone. The poor horse was something of an emotional wreck, as every time the owner took out her other horse he would run along the fence wearing himself out. She sent him to me for a few weeks to see what I could do with him.

This poor horse paced and paced all day. I put him in a

big yard next to the round yard where I was working all day, and I fed him as much hay as he wanted. On the first day, he paced and paced and paced. Each evening, his owner would ring up asking if he had stopped pacing yet. Day one, no change. Day two, pretty much the same. On day four he finally calmed down. I sensed that as an emotional, insecure kind of horse, he needed to work out for himself how to become calm, even if it took four days of pacing. While that sounds like being cruel to be kind, the horse needed to learn for himself. If I had got in the way, he would have learned only a little about how to calm himself, instead of really learning he was OK and safe.

When horses pace like that, they go into a mental space or zone where they don't really think properly. This horse would pace and pace, then after a while he would snap out of it for half an hour, then he'd remember and start pacing again. Like all the horses I worked with, he also spent a lot of time with me doing groundwork, which helped to reinforce the habit of thinking. When horses or people think, things are never as bad as they feel. Over time, I really believe he was grateful to get it out of his system. Horses thank us for our patience with them, especially when they're working through, or getting past, a challenging behaviour. Imagine if we could do that with people—come in and release all that tension, worry and baggage, then send them off full of confidence again.

That horse gained so much confidence and, in the end, once he was over his worries, his owner had a much better horse.

I had a lot of horses like him during that time. While most of them had predictable behaviours, not all did. One of my clients was a woman who'd had a horse for two weeks and couldn't ride it because she couldn't put the bridle on it. I went out to her property to teach her to get the horse to drop its head, and within about ten minutes I was able to get the bridle on. Afterwards I suggested she practise putting the bridle on before I left, and I said I'd show her again one more time.

Horses thank us for our patience with them, especially when they're working through, or getting past, a challenging behaviour.

As I got the horse to lower its head I noticed something wasn't right about its eye. Then suddenly it brought its head up, then blacked out and fell over with a huge crash. I leapt out of the way, and the horse stood up and came right. A few minutes later, when we had each caught our breath, I tried lowering the horse's head again to put the bridle on and the same thing happened. Once again I just managed to jump away and avoid being crushed.

Naturally, I suggested the owner get the vet out, and possibly the chiropractor. When the vet came out and lifted the horse's tail the same thing almost happened again. It turned out the horse was chronically sore through its back and when its head got to a certain height—as when it lifted its head quickly to avoid the bridle—it blacked out because of the extraordinary and unbearable pain.

Over the years I've had three or four horses who blacked out because of pain. There have been epileptic horses, too, though usually they become horses who can't be ridden because you never know when they might have a fit.

At this time I had three or four of my own horses, plus all the horses I was working with, and while I was keen to help every horse who came my way, I was also living on chip sandwiches and tomato sauce for dinner. One day my girlfriend said to me, 'Why don't you just sell your horses?' because she knew I was spending four hours a day or more on Rock, Pamper and my other horses. It had never occurred to me I could or should sell them—I just assumed these horses would be with me always—but I saw what she was saying, and that I would never be able to get ahead if I had so many mouths to feed.

It was hard, as Pamper and Rock had been with me from the beginning, but I sold Pamper to someone down near Nelson. A client who lived nearby had often said if I ever wanted to sell Rock, she'd be interested in buying him. So I said she could buy him for $500, thinking at least he'd still be close. I had been hoping to use my own horses for the leadership courses I wanted to run, but I wasn't at that stage yet, and in the daily choice between feeding the horses and feeding myself, the horses always won. I really had to focus on getting the business going.

It broke my heart to sell Rock, and two and a half years later, when his owner called and asked me if I wanted him back, I didn't hesitate. By then I was getting the corporate courses up and running. Though we hadn't been together in all that time, on the very first day we were reunited we did a demonstration and it was as if no time had passed at all. He probably did the best demonstration ever. Man, he was fast! It was pretty clear to both of us we were happy to be back together again, and now we were going to get out and show people what horses can teach us about ourselves.

It broke my heart to sell Rock, and two and a half years later, when his owner called and asked me if I wanted him back, I didn't hesitate.

IN 2002 I WAS living up in Waikanae in a little beach cottage with Jakey, my old dog. Jakey was great with the horses. He would wait outside the yard all day while I was working, and when he saw me give the horse a final rub he would come racing up because he knew the day was over. If he saw a horse pawing the ground he would run over to it and give it a little attitude and let it know it was out of line. It was so funny to see him trotting back to the edge of the round pen just grinning. If the horse dared to paw again Jakey would run back up to it again. I'm sure he thought he could do my job better than I could!

This was the year in which I met a woman who changed the course of the path I was on. She was a journalist, and I met her when she was going out with a friend of mine. When I told her I was a horse whisperer she was full of questions, and I was naturally happy to answer. Her relationship with my friend only lasted a few weeks, and she gave me a call on New Year's Eve, suggesting we get together for a drink. A few days later she came up from Wellington to see me with the horses.

After that we would get together from time to time, then a bit later she moved up the coast to a friend's property where there were some horses. By then she knew all about my dream of building up a property where I could do all the things I wanted to do, and she really supported my vision. We started looking for a property together, as she had inherited some money which made it possible for her to buy something.

At the same time, we went up to Gisborne to buy some station-bred horses we were going to get started and then bring down to Wellington to sell. We took two trips like this and each time we brought back six horses. We rented a cottage on Wainui Beach in Gisborne for these trips, and we'd go to the local feed shops and ask who would be good contacts for these kinds of horses. We were looking for good solid horses we could work with, and also building relationships with some of the people up there.

One of the people we met was Murray Candy, who had quite a bit of land in the high country there. He had good relationships with a lot of people in the area, so he got some of the horses from the back country and worked them for a while on his land, then he on-sold them. Murray had a great way about him, and I really respected the way he was with the horses.

One night, when we were staying with Murray, I saw a big, beautiful 17-hand Paint horse in a paddock. I asked him about the horse a couple of times, and each time he would change the subject or try to distract me. Eventually I cornered him and asked, 'So, what about this horse over here?'

'His name's Asshole,' Murray said. 'He's not a mongrel, just an asshole. Actually that's not even his name; it's just what he is. He's a bloody asshole of a horse. He's knocked me over a few times when we've been mustering. He's hard to catch and he's a bugger to shoe.'

He told me Asshole had been something of a personal project. He'd taken him out mustering cattle a few times and when the poor horse saw cows he just stood there and shook. He had obviously been beaten up pretty badly around them in the past.

'I will say, though,' Murray added, 'he's got the biggest heart of any horse I've ever ridden. He just goes and goes and goes all day.' After seeing me work with the horse for a little while he said, 'I think you get him and might do well with him, so take him.'

I did. I took him back to Wellington and we called him Mojo. He was such a big, beautiful fellow, but I foolishly put him in a large paddock on the first day and then had to spend an hour and a half just trying to catch him. The next day it took half an hour, but within two weeks I had him so he practically ran up to greet me the minute he saw me at the gates. I loved creating that relationship with him as he really did have one of the biggest hearts of any horse I've ever met.

Mojo liked to play rough with the other horses, and I'd see them truly horsing around in the paddock. Mojo would be getting down on his knees and nibbling legs, then the next minute he would be rearing up and cantering off. I love creating a freeing environment, taking these sorts of horses and totally turning them around into happy horses with fantastic attitudes. Horses like Mojo, who have seen the bad side of people, will do anything for you when you treat them right and gain their trust.

Horses like Mojo, who have seen the bad side of people, will do anything for you when you treat them right and gain their trust.

When he first arrived I did my usual health checks and we found he had a sore back, which I think was why Murray had found him so difficult to catch. He knew it was probably going to hurt. I was glad we were able to figure him out and help him. He was one of the great outcomes of those trips to Gisborne.

A few months after this, my partner and I were touring around down in Nelson with her mother, who was visiting from the UK. In the Saturday paper my partner noticed a 20-hectare property for sale up the coast from Wellington which looked pretty appealing. The auction was that week, so I went back up to have a look at the property to see if it would be suitable for the courses I wanted to run.

I can still picture it as it was the first time I saw it. The place was rundown, but it had the most stunning outlook, and I could visualise what it could look like if we put some energy into it. I knew it would need a lot of work, but it would be worth it. My partner bought the property and we began two years of incredibly hard work to bring it up to the level necessary for the work we wanted to do. Working paddock by paddock, I fenced and developed the whole property. My partner was great about putting money into the business and making sure we had the best of everything we needed—post and rail fences, a developed racetrack, beautiful buildings.

In the evenings I would stand outside having a smoke, and I could picture what would come next. My dreams were starting to become reality. We had complementary skills, with my partner's background in journalism and marketing, and my experience with horses. It was all coming together.

While we were developing the property I was still working with horse after horse, and I was probably becoming a bit burnt out. We had over twenty horses on the property at the time, and just looking after them was a tremendous amount of work. Then as the business developed and we added buildings, we were able to host weddings, demonstrations and corporate groups.

It took us five years to get to where I felt that we were achieving our dream. The property was beautiful, the courses were going well, there was growing interest in our work overseas, and my son Luca had come into the world. On the outside, I had achieved the dream. But on the home front, our relationship wasn't so good. The project was so big we both had more than enough to do every day, but we didn't necessarily click well with each other. Maybe we never really had, or maybe it was the pressure of trying to do so much that made the cracks in our relationship start to widen.

If horses are good avoiders, so are humans, and for a long time I didn't want to address the problems I knew were there. I poured myself into my work. Eventually, though, my relationship with my partner fell apart and I had to make some hard choices. In a way I had it all, but I didn't have what I really wanted. And again I think this is where relationships matter so much, whether they're with horses or people. If you're not happy in your relationships, then all the rest doesn't really matter.

In the end, I had to walk away from it all—the business that had been my dream, the land, the whole thing. Not my son, though. I knew we would never again live together as a whole family, but I was, and still am, deeply involved in his life. I went through a dark spell, having to move back home, starting over, still running a business with someone who was really angry with me. I knew I had made some choices that had hurt other people, but they had changed the situation to something more honest and true.

One of the things I've learned from horses, though, is about forgiveness. And they will always be there for you, no matter what. I gave less than my best to them during those dark years as I didn't have the emotional energy to give them more. They showed me their healing side in a way I often see when we work with troubled kids. They listened to me. They accepted maybe I was going through the motions for a while. They let me work through what I needed to work through and, amazingly, they forgave me. In the end, it was the horses who got me through the darkest times. They taught me something about relationships I still can't really put into words, but that's why the waters between us run so deep, and on winter days I make sure they're rugged up warm with plenty to eat.

One of the things I've learned from horses, though, is about forgiveness. And they will always be there for you, no matter what.

They listened to my secrets and they forgave me. And in true horse spirit, they taught me how to put one foot in front of the other and to keep going. I wonder where they learned that?

EVER SINCE KIWI, SOME part of me has been looking for that racehorse I know is out there, just waiting for me to turn him around. And it was during this period of my life, when my circumstances changed so much, I thought I had found him at last. It was one of the things that gave me a sense of hope. I had been starting to make a name for myself fixing problem racehorses, but I was still in search of *the one*—a well-known problem horse who had real ability but whom I could turn around and take all the way.

That was when King Guru walked into my life. Maybe his name was appropriate, because he turned out to be a teacher of a different kind, one I never expected to meet.

I had been at the track watching the horses one day when I saw a horse being scratched at the barrier because he wouldn't enter the starting gates. He had been listed as the favourite to win, so I knew there was something to follow up there. The next day I called his trainer and suggested I might be able to solve King Guru's problems. I believe we have to make our own luck and create opportunities in life, rather than sit back and wait, so I have always been very proactive in this way. The trainer said he didn't really think it was a major issue, but he would mention me to the owners.

A few days later the trainer called and told me the owners had decided to send King Guru to another trainer. I watched and waited, and a little while later, when I was once again at the track, I saw King Guru's name come up again, scratched at the barrier. Clearly the problem wasn't being resolved.

This time I gave the owner a call. He was open to the idea of me working with King Guru, but had already promised the horse to a trainer in Auckland. I really felt for the horse, as having three trainers in rapid succession meant they would have tried all kinds of things to fix his problem. At that point in his career King Guru had had six race-day starts, with two wins, a second, and then a third, fourth and fifth. For a horse with so much going wrong it seemed there was still a whole lot that must have been going right.

Unfortunately, though, he had now been barred from racing because of his manners and behaviour. He would have to undergo two trials and satisfy the racing stewards before he would be allowed to start in a race again. In Auckland the trainers tried all kinds of things, including blindfolds, which I found surprising in this day and age. They were able to get him to pass one of the barrier trials, but he failed at the second. It was then I received a phone call from the owner asking if I was still interested in working with him. Of course I was.

I proposed to the owner that he make me half owner of the horse. At that point he was worth nothing because he couldn't race, but I didn't believe he was going to stay that way. I said I would train him and that the owner would pay nothing towards the training fees until King Guru had passed his two barrier trials and been reinstated. The owner was hopeful and believed in me, and the deal was struck.

A week later King Guru arrived, and what a beautiful horse he was. He stood 17-hands high and was all bay except for a white star in the middle of his forehead. He had a strong, well-proportioned body and good legs. It was a joy just to look at him. I knew, though, given all the physical and mental stresses of being through three different trainers in a year, the issues associated with the gates, plus the fact that by then it was winter, the best course of action would be to give him a break. I let the owner know that was the plan, and all I wanted for the first six weeks was for King Guru to have the chance to relax. No more pressure or stress.

I had a big 4-hectare rolling paddock saved up with knee-high grass for him. I double-rugged him and put him out there with four other horses to keep him company, fed him twice a day, gave him as much hay as he wanted, and a brush once a week. King Guru thought life was pretty good, and he always bowled up to have a good rub and to say hi whenever I was in the paddock.

I loved watching him with the other horses. Within two days he was the boss man, and that was good to see. There's something really special about seeing those dominant, tough horses in their own world.

His six weeks of holiday came and went quickly, and as the days got longer I moved him to another paddock with a new mate and started running him through my system. He responded beautifully. His teeth were done, his body checked, and we began to get into some fitness. It helped that his attitude was just excellent. He was simply a very happy horse. Every day I rode a lead horse and led him out all over the farm, around the roads and out to the beach. He especially loved the beach.

After six weeks of work he was looking a million dollars. By then he had developed a trusting relationship with me and a strong bond. He loved all the praise, was seeking it, and had a bright, happy eye. By then we had a set of four gates, and I decided it was time to take King Guru down to have his first look at them. I led him up to the gates for a sniff and thought I would give him a pick of the grass for five minutes to ease him in nice and slowly. He wasn't so keen on that! Even though we had been together for the past three months, this was the first time I saw the other side of him. I thought he would just walk through the gates calmly and easily, but that wasn't the case at all. It took me about twenty minutes of gentle work with him to get him to go through the gates.

We made good progress, and as we walked up the hill that day I can remember feeling happy and excited that we were slowly starting to move him along. I knew everything that needed to be done with him so he could be presented at those trials for a new barrier certificate. He was now feeling fantastic under saddle, and I knew I had a horse who was more than capable of going out and cleaning up in a few races. The thought of that alone felt wonderful.

I left the farm after lunch that Saturday with my son, Luca, as we were heading down to Wellington for the rest of the weekend. The horses and I had Sunday off. Or so I thought.

Late on the Sunday afternoon, I received a phone call from my former partner, now my business partner, who was doing the night-time feeds and checking on the horses. She said it was pouring with rain and she was going to feed the horses a little earlier than usual. It was only four o'clock.

Ten minutes later the phone rang again: 'King Guru's got blood all down his leg. I'm calling the vet.'

As I put the phone down I thought, 'Oh please . . . Any horse but him . . . '

The phone rang again. 'The vet's here. King Guru's broken his leg. I'll let you know what he says.'

I waited. Two very long minutes later the phone rang again. 'King Guru's dead.'

I was shattered. I drove the hour from Wellington to the farm feeling sick, but I wanted to see him. When I got there, I could see what had happened. The ground underfoot was wet, he had been having a good old play in the paddock, and had slipped and broken his leg. My poor big fella.

King Guru taught me that nothing is for certain and that one day you're on a high and the next day can be a deep low.

Even though it was still raining, I went and sat next to him in the paddock for hours; it felt like days. I was crushed, because we had been spending so much time together and I had been so excited about what we could achieve together. And now he was dead. It took me a few tries before I could finally pick up the phone and call the owner.

He hadn't set out to be my guru, but in some ways King Guru taught me that nothing is for certain and that one day you're on a high and the next day can be a deep low. His death was one of those deep lows.

I have never found another horse like him—a horse with a certain X factor that everyone else has given up on—but I hope he's still out there somewhere. If you know that horse, will you let me know about him? We're waiting for each other.

The leader within

HORSES AS TEACHERS

On a hot February afternoon ten of New Zealand's best sports coaches are in the arena below my house, each holding a horse loosely by the lead rope. Above us is the outline of Coronet Peak and below the whole valley spreads out, with rolling tussock-coloured hills and the crags of the Remarkables in the hazy distance. The horses are a little bored, perhaps, and the coaches are trying not to appear nervous.

I know none of the coaches wants to look foolish or lose face. I also know what they're about to do is going to show them how to be better leaders, so even though there'll be some discomfort during the process, the takeaways are too good for them not to engage. At least that's what every coach and every corporate executive who's taken my leadership course over the last ten years has said.

So now I tell them, 'This is the best opportunity you might ever have to learn something about why you do or don't get the results you want with your athletes. Your horse is going to be showing you things you've probably never seen before—or things you've hoped not to have to see. Either way, you're a team, and I'm going to show you a few tasks, and you and your horse are going to do them together. We'll film you, then in an hour or so we'll go up to the house and we can all have a look at the video together.'

Earlier I talked about why horses are the ideal animals for learning about leadership. Because of the structures of their bands and groups, horses are always looking for the best leader. And just like humans, there are horses who think they are the leader, make a lot of fuss and demand a lot of attention, but at the end of the day the leader of the band is the horse the other horses follow . . . not the horse who says, 'Look at me!'

Our world isn't too different, and when horses and humans get together one of the two is going to have to be the leader. Personally, I'd rather be the leader than be subject to whatever the horse has in mind for me to do, so by nature our relationship with horses is already a relationship about leadership.

My dream of connecting horses and courses on leadership really started to gel about fifteen years ago. At the time, I was working with a young woman's horse in Greytown once every fortnight. I was there around lunchtime one day and her father happened to be visiting. He was a big South African guy who I knew worked in professional development. He stood a little away from me and watched very seriously for the last twenty minutes of my work with the horse. When we were finished, he and his daughter invited me in for lunch.

His group of national managers had learned more in three hours with the horses than in three days in the usual classroom course.

'You know, this is fascinating,' he said, with real excitement in his voice, and then he proceeded to ask a whole raft of questions. Turned out he ran a company called Vision and Leadership, and he said what I was doing with the horses was what he was doing with people. When we put together the concept of bringing the people and the horses together, we could both see how powerful the transformative potential of it was. So we set up some half-day courses for his people where everyone had a chance to work with a horse. At the time he was working with the NZ Dairy Board and NZ Pharmaceuticals. From there, I began doing courses with many other people, and with each course I got feedback that helped me, and ultimately the people with whom I've worked, to hone the courses to be better and better.

I was really inspired by the feedback from some of the early guys, like the head of branch banking at ASB Bank who told me his group of national managers had learned more in three hours with the horses than in three days in the usual classroom course. I knew I was onto something good.

What's been fun for me is that I've worked with people in the field of personal development and leadership even though it's not the area I've come from. Sometimes people think I'm offering courses to make them good horse people. I'm not. I'm offering courses to make people good leaders, using horses as a teaching tool. The horses are emotional mirrors and they give immediate, honest feedback in a way that nothing and no one else can. I think it's important to remember, too, that their wants and needs are completely different from ours. They're so profoundly sensitive they can read us like a book and there's no way to hide from what they see.

The horses are emotional mirrors and they give immediate, honest feedback in a way that nothing and no one else can.

The power of this concept was very evident on one of the first courses we did. One of the men on the team was very arrogant, so we set him up with Bolt, my thoroughbred demonstration horse who had gone from being a bucking horse to a winner. There was a real contest of wills, and they were just at each other all day long. Eventually all the other team members were cheering for Bolt and hoping he would teach the guy a lesson, since he never seemed to learn it from the people on his team.

Working with horses provides an avenue for feedback, the likes of which most people never see. This is not some performance review on a piece of paper, but real live feedback from a horse saying, 'If you keep doing what you're doing, you're not going to get results.' How good is that?

Why does it work? Horses are the perfect mirror. They don't mirror to us who we say we are, they mirror to us the energy we bring to them, the attitude we bring, the clarity of our communication, and the boundaries we do or don't set up. Above all, they test our capacity for consistency and whether or not we truly walk the talk. That is why they are so useful for coaches, executives and leaders who are experiencing a gap between what they'd like to achieve and the results they are actually getting. The horse shows you what it is you're not seeing in your leadership style because it simply won't do what you've asked.

At the beginning of our courses each person is paired with an appropriate horse, based on information we've been given on their strengths, weaknesses and challenges. For example, if I know they've had trouble with communication at work, I might give them a horse who is either highly responsive to everything or a little slow and not responsive at all, so they can work through the whole range of subtleties in that area. In the past we used to have Hontis, a stubborn little white donkey on the farm who had attitude with a capital A. I would often pair him with a person who'd been known for bullying staff, to see how the two of them were going to negotiate this relationship. No matter what, every horse, or donkey, has something to teach.

Just like in the groundwork I do with my horses, the very first step is to establish a safe distance so the horse knows that while you can step into its space, it can't step into yours. This is the most important piece of horse safety, as naturally you want to make sure everyone feels they have some control in the relationship, and that 'No' means 'No' when you don't want a horse to go any further than your outstretched palm.

It never ceases to amaze me how strong the leadership lesson is for some people in this very first activity. But really, with an outstretched arm, the word 'Stop', and then clear praise when it's done right, you've got about twenty lessons in real-life leadership. Some people, as their horse comes towards them and they have their hand up saying 'Stop', will take a step back at the same time and then another step back. I often think that if a horse could laugh then it would, knowing it had literally walked all over someone who said 'No' but didn't mean it.

And how often is this true at work? So here, with the horse, is an opportunity to try again, to work out what it feels like to stand your ground, establish a true boundary, not be afraid to tell the horse to step back when it steps into your space, and to communicate clearly with both body and words exactly what you mean and where you both stand.

When people are hesitant, or they don't know for sure what they want, the horse picks it up. Seeing their weakness, the horse might start to step in and try to intimidate a little. It's really no different from what happens in the workplace sometimes.

When we watch the videos of the first hour of the course there is often a bit of shared laughter, because in truth almost no one is good at this at the beginning. Some people are still getting over their past fear of horses, and some are nervous about how their colleagues will see them. Watching the video together always helps as it seems seeing everyone 'warts and all' inspires a desire to help each other get better, and really creates a shared experience within the group. The video analysis is a really powerful way to make personal changes. I might tell someone they are a bit flat, to pick up their energy and carry themselves with real purpose. Often people think they are already doing it, until they see them-selves on video and realise they aren't doing it at all.

When we go out to the arena for the second round, there is always a marked difference. Seeing yourself be walked over by a horse has a huge impact, and most people come back and begin to develop greater inner strength of some kind. This is where I think their leader within begins to emerge. And once they've mastered this first step, there are building blocks upward. Leadership is just as often found in nuance as it is found in the big, grand gestures. In fact, I tend to believe it's found almost completely in the small.

Over the span of two days, as people work one on one with their horses, we talk about what I see as the nine princi-ples of leadership, which engagement with the horses seems to bring out in powerful and personal ways.

The nine principles are:

1. Relationships: Valuing the strength of relationships.
2. Communication: Verbal and non-verbal.
3. Clarity and Consistency: Boundaries, goals and expectations, standards, alignment of instructions and messages, follow-through.
4. Feedback: Praise vs shame/avoidance.
5. Honesty and Humility: You just can't fake it.
6. Building Achievable Success: If you're not succeeding, break the task down into small steps that are achievable, then move to bigger tasks from there. You can always make something smaller.
7. Embodied Energy: Physical presence, confidence, projection, energy up and down.
8. Commitment: Persistence, sticking to it, and believing in what you're both doing together.
9. Appreciation: When the task is finished, making sure you celebrate the success and appreciate everyone's involvement in it.

From what I can tell, these same principles could be applied to teaching, to parenting, to marriages, or just about anything that involves at least two beings and a common or shared goal.

I should add, too, that though the words get used interchangeably these days, especially in the corporate world, the words 'manager' and 'leader' mean very different things. 'Manager' actually comes from the horse world. Back in the sixteenth century, to manage literally meant 'to handle a horse' (*manus* is the Latin word for hand, and 'manager' came to us from Italian). In contrast, to 'lead' or be a 'leader' was closer to how horses themselves behave, where a leader guides others. I like to think of people in strong positions as being more like excellent guides than generic horse handlers. Or maybe, in an ideal world, they can be both. At any rate, they begin with the first and most important of all qualities—the valuing of a relationship.

Every horse I meet knows I am glad to meet it. I like to think every person I meet feels the same way. When we meet a person for the first time, we look them in the eye and we often shake hands. How often have you learned something surprising about a person from their handshake? Maybe they look strong but when their hand meets yours it's cold and clammy, or they don't greet you fully but leave a limp fish in your hand instead of something that feels robust. That little bit of non-verbal communication can tell you a lot about whether they are going through the motions or are genuinely glad to meet you and hoping to get to know you better. What we say verbally and what we say non-verbally are of equal strength, with horses or with people.

With horses, the first few moments and the first activity we do together are the equivalent of a good handshake and the start of a conversation. Our eyes reveal so much about where our attention lies. When you meet someone and they shake your hand but look over your shoulder at someone else, you know they aren't too interested in you. Similarly, if a horse is looking away from you, you know it's trying to avoid you. The question becomes, how are you going to bridge that gap and build a relationship?

With horses, the first few moments and the first activity we do together are the equivalent of a good handshake and the start of a conversation.

Just like shaking hands when you meet someone, you're probably going to reach out and touch your horse. You might rub it on the forehead. It might take a step back if you come at it too quickly or with too much force, or it might be really glad to feel your touch and to know there's nothing dangerous there. Every step of the way, your horse, just like a person, is trying to work out how committed you are to this relationship. It's asking, do you really care if I succeed at what you're asking me to do?

In the workplace, this is a big one. Staff know when you can't remember their names, and they value a leader who does. They remember who treats them like a person and who treats them like a replaceable widget, or just another in a long line of people who have taken that role before. Good results have everything to do with good relationships—people, like horses, want to feel valued. Many people think they don't have time to invest in those relationships, but it's actually far more efficient to do so. Taking a small amount of time to learn someone's name and praising them when they have done good work is much more productive than trying to manage someone who senses you really don't care.

ENERGY IS A REALLY important area of non-verbal communication. It is a big factor in how people, and horses, react to us, and it's one of the areas where working with horses can be most revealing. Your energy is something you can't fake, but it's something you can learn to control once you have seen how it works.

Years ago, when I was working up in Waikanae, I met a guy who was a prime example of someone who had no idea of the effect of his energy on his horses. Ray Diamond was one of the most high-energy people I ever met. Talked a blue streak. He called me because he had been ripped off. He had left some horses with a trainer to break in and feed, but when he went back he found the horses hadn't been looked after well and were just skin and bone.

Two of Ray's horses, Captain and Glenn, were Clydesdales, beautiful big horses. Ray loved these horses, but he had real trouble controlling them. The first time I went out to see him he was yelling, 'Captain, Captain, stand up!' He was completely unaware of his high energy, and these two huge horses were completely wiped out by it. I'd say to him, 'Ray, Ray, just chill out . . .' and send him off to do something else. His energy set the horses off and they were on constant high alert when he was around.

The first thing I did was work with Ray to help him learn how to quiet himself around the horses. The way he did this was by taking on small tasks with them and building up a relationship quietly but consistently. He fed his horses every night, which meant he saw them every single day and they all got used to each other—it wasn't Christmas morning every time he saw them. They became daily companions and he could quiet himself to match them. Today, he's got a great relationship with those horses. I think he has fed them every night for the last five years, which means he's hardly had a day apart from them. He talks of having been transformed by his experiences with the horses. I can believe it. And when I see him now, I am always telling him he is too chilled out and needs to pick up his energy again. Ray has also become a good mate.

I've seen energy work in three ways with people. First you have the high-energy people like Ray. They bring that high energy to the horse and it feels like a frenetic force-field. The horse can barely take in what you're telling it because it's so busy feeling all the heightened energy. Horses read your energy in the speed of your movement, when you're making hand gestures that are all over the show, talking fast, and pulling on the lead rope so you're moving them too quickly through whatever it is you've asked of them.

What are they going to do in the face of all that energy? Well, they're either going to slow right down because they can't figure out what all the buzzing is about or they're going to get nervous. Now there are two big nervous creatures in the same space, neither of them quite listening to the other before trying to move on to the next thing.

The second kind of energy is the complete opposite. These are the people who don't bring any energy to the relationship at all. It's like having Eeyore come to your party, because there never seems to be anything that's worth getting motivated about. A horse mirroring this kind of energy is going to do exactly what you imagine it would do: nothing.

Horses are big animals, and when they stand there doing nothing it's pretty obvious, especially if you're in the middle of a course where the other horses are all responding. This is a horse who is thinking you're maybe a fly. Or perhaps a gust of wind. There's just nothing there for it to get interested or excited about.

A lot of the time these are people who are afraid of horses, and their fear makes them take their energy way down, too far down. They have to gain the confidence to bring their energy back up again. One of the ideas I offer is that it's a bit like being a teenager who is trying to get into a bar. Even when you know you're underage, if you fake it and put on a bit of a swagger you can give the impression you belong. After a while you relax back into yourself and then you're fine. It's the 'fake it till it feels real' approach. This doesn't usually take long. There's probably a translation to the workplace, where no one really wants to be there on Monday morning; it's up to the boss or the leader to fake it until everyone is back into the swing of things.

The third kind of energy is the one we are hoping for. This is the consistent energy that says: 'I'm here and I'm keen to get our goals met.' I see this as a steady energy. It's the one that can take in the highs and lows of the horse's energy more easily because no matter what the horse offers, you come back to it with consistency. If you want the horse to move faster, you can raise your energy or increase the pressure you are putting on it (I do this with a lot of clicking), and if you want it to slow, you can slow your own energy right down. Many people in long-term leadership roles have this natural consistent energy. It makes other people feel safe, and they are able to gauge whether a task requires ramping up or slowing down.

The All Blacks coach Steve Hansen, who has taken my course, is an outstanding example of this third kind of energy. Because his range of emotion is usually very stable, when he does break into a big smile or, equally, look very serious, his players read that very clearly. Most of the time, what he gives them is what they need most—consistency.

I'm always surprised the concept of consistency gets so little attention in the world of leadership, or in most worlds, in fact, since it's the foundation of just about everything in the work I do. It's noticeable how often it is lacking in parenting and relationships, and when people complain they're not getting the responses or results they want, I always wonder why they don't go back to this one. It's my gold standard.

In working with horses, nothing creates more safety for them, nothing creates more loyalty from them, than consistency. That way, they always know where they stand. The significance of consistency flows on from energy and valuing relationships. If you show up to a relationship with the energy to sustain it, then the next step is to show you're going to be there no matter what. That's where consistency comes in.

Consistency has two main functions. First, it reinforces that you say what you mean. Second, it says you accept there will be ups and downs created by circumstances, but you will always present yourself as the same reliable person. No dramas.

In working with horses, nothing creates more safety for them, nothing creates more loyalty from them, than consistency. That way, they always know where they stand.

In my courses, I find that people are happy to praise their horse, but they are inconsistent in correcting negative behaviours. Horses, especially at the outset of a relationship, are like kids on the first night with a new babysitter. They want to see what they can get away with. They really want to see what you're made of. I suspect they're hoping you'll be the kind of leader they feel they can trust. I don't know if horses hope, but I like to think they do, and I'd hate to let them down.

Praise is important, essential, and I'll talk more about it in a moment. But consistency is almost more important as it lets a horse, or a co-worker, know that this is always how we do things. If the first time you're working with your horse you ask it to stop and it does, that's great. But it doesn't mean the horse has mastered that concept and now you can move on. You've got to do it again. And again, and again. And every time the horse does what it was asked to do, you have to meet it with consistent praise. But every time it chooses not to do what was asked, it has to know you noticed and it's not OK. Try again.

Consistency is in large part about saying 'I notice', and that you're willing to be the bad guy if necessary to make sure any negative behaviour doesn't take root. Children understand this inherently, and while they will try to play a parent who they see as less consistent, they will rarely try to get a consistent parent to change his or her tune. The boundary is there and it is real. Whether it's kids, horses, partners or workmates, we are always happier when basic boundaries are in place and we all know where we stand.

When I give demonstrations with the horses, this is one of the areas people often notice and comment on. After I've shown the group a few things with Chance or Rock, I might be talking to the audience. Naturally, the horses rather like being the centre of attention, and if they find they're not, they may start nudging in or doing something to get themselves noticed. Even though I'm talking to the crowd, I don't let the horses get away with anything they aren't allowed to do normally. So I stop and correct them, and then I carry on with the talk. Consistency really does mean all the time, not just on special occasions, otherwise it just confuses the horse.

I think they like it, too. It's their way of testing me to see if I'm true. And I want to be true in every relationship, so consistency is the way of showing that your words and your actions are all one.

Our words are our power, and this is true in working with horses and people. Often people will ask me if I think horses understand the words we say. I don't know if they understand all of them, but they are incredibly intelligent creatures so if we always say the same thing with the same action, they will start to respond to voice commands. But it's important to be very clear and not to overwhelm them with a whole monologue when we want them to do something simple: clarity is essential.

Clarity allows everyone to know what the common goals are, and to know when they have been achieved. It's about simple directions, clear goals, and alignment of instructions and messages. I find the people on my courses who struggle with clarity are often the ones who are in a great rush. Perhaps they want to show they can do whatever was asked of them faster and better than anyone else. What usually happens is they overwhelm their poor horse with too much information. The horse has no idea what they mean, so they either try to do everything at once or they just stand there and do nothing.

There's nothing like a horse to tell you when you haven't communicated well. And when they reflect this back to us it can be pretty painful. This is the place where people get angry, lose the plot, and blame the horse for being purpose-fully stubborn, difficult or getting in the way, when really it is they who haven't communicated clearly enough. But what about the people with whom they work? When a task has not been done properly, is it possible there's been a lack of clarity rather than a purposeful desire not to carry out the task? Many people find the missing piece of their leadership style right here in this reflection that the horses offer so well.

There's nothing like a horse to tell you when you haven't communicated well.

Thoroughness is a part of this, too. Some people get bored with a task very quickly. So while the horse might not have mastered the skill yet, the person wants to rush ahead because they want to do something new instead of doing something right. Creating an atmosphere where thoroughness and consistency are more important than novelty makes a huge difference in the long run.

ONE OF THE MOST important things with regard to how we communicate with horses is praise. I believe everyone benefits from praise, because it says 'I noticed' and 'Thank you'. Horses, like humans, want to be noticed, but often they don't want to be too noticed. I also find this with many of the young people with whom I work. If they've had bad experiences in the past, where being noticed led to being told to do something painful, or to confusing circumstances, they will have developed the art of becoming invisible. Horses who have suffered at people's hands can have the same attitude, where initially they don't want too much attention because they associate attention with something frightening or unpredictable.

Praise used well, though, is a beautiful thing. It takes down walls. It strengthens relationships. It lets in gratitude. It conveys to the horse, or the person, that you noticed them and you appreciated they did just what they were asked to do. It builds confidence.

Praise doesn't have to be effusive; in fact, it's a lot better if it isn't. I tend to go with 'Good girl' or 'Good boy' with the horses I work with. I give them a good rub and praise them when they have done just what was asked of them. If the work is shoddy, half done, or still in need of improvement, I might let them know their try was 'just average'. They don't get praise for doing nothing—praise only works when it is genuine.

Have you ever received a performance review where there's some category checked off that doesn't even apply to you? False praise is actually a negative reinforcer, because it conveys an absence of interest. Praising at the wrong time usually tells me someone is feeling awkward and is not sure what to do, so they praise instead.

As a horse is learning something, I'll praise the small steps along the way. Sometimes the horse might not have got it all exactly right, but I know it's trying so I fall back on Ray Hunt's notion of 'Reward the smallest change and the slightest try'. It's a way of encouraging someone who wants to do better, even if they're not all the way there yet.

Some people who don't know how to use praise well fall into the belief that people don't need praise. They should intrinsically know when they've done a good job, and if they've done a bad job they'll be met with either shaming or avoidance. Often there's a cultural belief that praising is inherently 'soft' or 'false' and creates weaker people or weaker systems. I know of no one for whom a bit of well-earned praise won't create a greater desire to achieve more.

At the same time, we can overpraise. I often think back to the first public praise my grandfather ever gave me for my work with horses, when I was fifteen. He praised so little that when he did praise it meant a lot to me; in fact, it probably helped to set me on my path. His praise said what I think good praise always says: 'I noticed you doing this well . . .' It meant the world to me then.

As a horse is learning something, I'll praise the small steps along the way.

I also believe in patience, or more specifically, patience coupled with confidence. I see this as the trait of a real leader. Good leaders believe in their teams and know they can achieve outcomes. While no one has the luxury of infinite time, effective leaders possess the patience that comes from knowing 'it takes as long as it takes' to ultimately get the outcome you desire.

Many of the people who come to us from the corporate

environment haven't been given the freedom to pursue this concept, and they often find it difficult to accept. The corporate clock makes a lot of people feel as though they don't have the freedom to let a person learn from their mistakes, or to use reverse psychology to teach them. There's an assumption that doing something quickly means it's being done right, which is not necessarily true. I believe that whether it's a horse who needs to take an hour the first time it gets into a float, or one like old Rock who forced me to spend a whole afternoon helping him get over having wet feet when we walked through a boggy paddock, the time invested in getting the small things right always pays off in the long run.

That's the challenge I love most about working with horses—I am trying to get an animal who has a mind of its own as tuned in, reliable and dependable as I can possibly get it.

It's about patience and confidence, and the fundamental belief that at the end of the day the lesson learned once and learned well won't have to be repeated over and over again. I believe in the horses I work with being 'bombproof', which means doing everything I can to make sure I can predict their reactions, no matter what the circumstances. That's the challenge I love most about working with horses—I am trying to get an animal who has a mind of its own as tuned in, reliable and dependable as I can possibly get it.

My hope is always that those who do my two-day course will have the opportunity to experience success once they are willing to believe the outcome they are asking for is achievable. They need only apply patience and confidence, and eventually they and the horse will get there. There's a deep sense of empowerment when the moment comes, and I love filming people at that point so they can see it in their own faces, too.

ONE OF THE CONCEPTS I introduce during the course seems quite obvious, but it's something we often forget. I call it 'Building achievable success', but really it's more like looking at a map when you're lost and saying, 'Go back to the last spot where you knew where you were and start again.'

When we work with the horses we move in steps that build from one skill to the next. So we begin with creating safety and boundaries, but in time we may want the horse to cross a bridge with us or participate in a confidence course with other horses. How do you build up that skill set so you know the horse will do what you've asked of it?

This is where many people succumb to the lure of rushing. They get a little confidence under their belt, the horse starts responding the way they want it to, and the tendency is to get ahead of themselves. In the early stages, when they don't really know what they're doing, they will do something over and over to get it right. But, then, with a little more experience and confidence, they start skipping steps and speeding things up, and that's usually when it all suddenly (and sometimes spectacularly) stops working. So what do they need to do? Go back to the last place where they were sure the horse had mastered the concept and start rebuilding.

A national swimming coach told me this was one of the most useful concepts he took away from the course. He has swimmers who come to him from other coaches all over the country, and he used to assume that because of the level at which they performed, they must have mastered all the basics. Sometimes, though, he would have an athlete who wasn't progressing as he had expected. Now, he says, he goes back to the basics with everyone when they come onto the team, so he can assess where they are really at and where they are going. 'It may look like a waste of time to someone on the outside,' he told me, 'but it saves me heaps of time in the long run.'

I have had the same experience with countless horses, and the more I do this kind of work the more I encourage people to rethink their relationship with time, because time spent in mastery is truly time spent only once.

A concept that's closely related to this is breaking tasks down into smaller components. Sometimes when a task is too complex the horse might be able to follow some of what you're asking of it, but not everything. When people find themselves hung up on getting a horse to do something quite complicated, I encourage them to break the task down into the smallest possible steps and then to exaggerate each step until they are sure the horse has truly understood. Again, this might sound obvious, but so often we forget to do it.

Another aspect of leadership that working with horses can reveal is the concept of commitment. Initially, most people are enthusiastic, and over the first couple of hours those who are seeing steady results are keen to continue. When we're ready to break for lunch they don't realise it's that time already—they're completely absorbed in their horse and the task they're involved in.

But for those for whom the morning has been a challenge, who are still trying to keep their horse at arm's length or have achieved far less than they had hoped, lunchtime can't come soon enough as they look for a way out. 'Hey, Andrew, I think the horse you gave me has some issues. What about setting me up with a different horse this afternoon?' I often wonder if their performance reviews talk about a lack of commitment, especially when it comes to relationships or long-term tasks where there are layers of difficulty rather than immediate outcomes.

Someone who lacks that commitment might feel frustrated, that they are falling behind the rest of the group, or suddenly decide the workshop is 'too hard' or 'stupid'. At the point where the toys are being thrown from the cot (and I have to say, this only happens about once a year) I usually let the person go through the whole range of emotions before I rein them in. How else are you going to get them to stop and ask themselves, if I do this in a course where I'm trying to get a horse to cross a little bridge, what am I going to do when it comes to getting my whole team to achieve its goals? Are they going to take their toys and go home every time things don't work out as planned?

Once the storm blows over, we start again. We go back to the last known place of mastery and work together to see if it's possible to get past it. Of course it is always possible, and everyone always does, but it's a very good way of finding out just how strong or deep their commitment is or isn't. In the workplace there is always something that is going to make someone say, 'I've had enough.' The question is, what does a leader do then? Do you let them leave? Do you give them space to come back? Do you feed frustration or starve it?

When the subject comes up during a course, we're able to talk about commitment to a task and often commitment to each other. Commitment is an essential part of any long-term relationship, whether it's with a horse or with one's partner or workmates.

The reason Rock and I perform so well together is the number of times we have tested our relationship—which did include those few years apart—and we both know I'll see him out of this world unless something happens to me first. We have shown up for each other during the hard times. We have been as stubborn as two creatures could be and have tested each other's will so many times that all we can do is laugh at each other now, but the end result is truly rock solid. The depth of one's capacity for commitment is something that may require testing from time to time. Leaders don't commit to everything—there's discernment involved in terms of what is worthwhile and makes sense—and not everything in life is of long duration, but knowing your own capacity for commitment without a doubt helps you to find your leader within.

THE LAST QUALITY I talk about in our courses is perhaps the hardest to teach, but as far as I can tell it's the one that distinguishes true leaders from all the rest. I've worked with a few of those truly inspiring leaders, and what makes them different is ultimately their humility and their honesty. All the best leaders always defer any compliments to someone else. They tend to accept the consequences of the actions of the whole team as their own, but they are not motivated as much by praise as they are by something more like personal integrity. They just want to do the job right, and they know what it means.

Knowing your own capacity for commitment without a doubt helps you to find your leader within.

Horses are the great leveller, and you learn from them never to take anything for granted. You could be on top of the world one day and the next they could break a leg, like King Guru. They don't care if you're wealthy or beautiful.

They don't care if you wield power on the world's stage or if you can decide another person's fate. They care if you notice them, you want the best for them, and you are honest with them. Promises to feed them and keep them warm mean nothing unless you show up every day to do so. Sharing the winner's circle with them is an absolute delight, there is no doubt, but knowing you'll be there on a rainy day with no one else around is probably far more important to them than sharing the limelight with them at the Melbourne Cup.

Horses mirror back honesty and humility beautifully. And the people I've seen who have been reflected that way in the horses' eyes generally take little notice of this. They simply look ahead to the next task, ask the horse if it's ready, and do what needs doing. At the end of the day, they are almost always the last ones to leave, too. They're the ones who stick around to help clean up, no matter who they are to the rest of the world. That's what I love about horses and people: if you treat them kindly, fairly, and with respect, they will do anything for you.

The person within

HORSES AS FRIENDS

On a hot summer's day, just after New Year, a white police car pulls up outside our house. Normally it might be a cause for worry, but on this morning we've been waiting for its arrival. Sam's been baking lemon cupcakes, and slapping my hands away when I try to make off with a couple before the arrival of our guests. Clicking at her does no good. I'm going to have to wait. I go outside and have a cigarette instead.

The doors of the police car open and out step Derek, a tall, fit policeman from Alexandra, and four fourteen-year-old girls. I can only begin to imagine what the conversation was like on the hour-long drive over from Central Otago, as only one of the four girls could be described as remotely quiet. Derek looks like he could use something stronger than the coffee we offer him, while the girls pile into the house and seat themselves on the sofas in the snug. Their hands are already hovering over the plate of cupcakes, and I'm grateful I manage to grab even one. It's good to be reminded just how quick and coordinated these girls are.

They are also troubled. That's why they are here on a summer's day instead of enjoying their school holidays. Each of them, for different reasons, has come to the attention of the law. As a result they have been put into a programme sponsored by REAP, the Rural Education Activities Programme. The programme is designed to give kids like these some opportunities to do something different before negative patterns and behaviours became too ingrained.

Programmes involving horses for therapy, healing and rehabilitation exist all over the world these days. They've had amazing success in helping people with disabilities and addictions, returning soldiers, and people facing all kinds of challenges. I became interested in them when I saw something on the internet about how prisoners in the US were being taught to break in mustangs, and the incredible results that were being achieved for both the people and the horses.

This was my fourth session with this group of girls on a course I call 'The Person Within'. It was my first group from Central Otago, but I had worked with troubled youth when we had the farm north of Wellington. I've done some rewarding work in my life, but working with these kids has been the most gratifying. In Wellington, I worked with eight young people twice a week for eight weeks. Some of these kids had been expelled from as many as ten schools, and some had their own social workers. The experiences they had with the horses, though, were nothing short of amazing.

I've done some rewarding work in my life, but working with these kids has been the most gratifying.

Around the same time as I was working with these kids, I was approached by the SPCA about doing a session with horses for the Epuni Care and Protection Residence. This is a Child, Youth and Family home for young people who, for a variety of reasons, can't live in the community for a while. In the past they'd had good success with taking in puppies and having them work with the kids, but they had never before done anything with horses. So I took some horses and worked with the kids there. The most life-changing event for me was when one of the boys, a sixteen-year-old who was severely autistic and had never spoken before, spoke for the first time following this experience. I was amazed, as I so often am, at the power of horses to help people unlock things inside them.

Following the success of both these programmes, I began doing some work with Prison Fellowship New Zealand, working with children who were having to deal with a parent being in prison. In each of these situations, the challenges the kids have had to face in their personal lives have often become a source of real strength as they work with their horses and gain a level of confidence they have never experienced before.

Many of these kids have learned through hard experience that people's feedback isn't always so trustworthy, but horses can't fake it—they are always honest about what they see.

There are layers of things happening between these kids and their horses which are hard to explain, but it's as if the horse gives them feedback that says, 'You're better than you think you are.' It is incredibly empowering. Many of these kids have learned through hard experience that people's feedback isn't always so trustworthy, but horses can't fake it—they are always honest about what they see—and they learn the real meaning of trust from their horse. I also find they are able to bring up to the surface some of their personal angers and frustrations and work them through in the safety of the paddock instead of erupting around other people where their feelings can set off a cascade of reactions. Just like the horses, out in the paddock there is room for them to buck until they're done bucking, so to speak. It's actually not too different, and there aren't too many places in their worlds where they can do that without it causing new problems for them.

So on this summer's day, after the girls have managed to make the lemon cupcakes disappear in record time, they sit on the two sofas giggling with the sugar rush while Sam flicks on the video from the previous session. Just like in the adult leadership courses, we use video so everyone can see how they're communicating with their horses, and we can do both self and group evaluation.

The first video is of Irene trying to get her horse to follow behind her and then stop on command. Her first attempt works well, then the next few attempts show Cool Guy, my spirited three-year-old thoroughbred, increasingly creeping into her space. Sam asks, 'Sian, can you tell us what you see in Irene's video?'

Of all the girls, Sian is the most reserved, and she is sitting on the edge of the sofa, a little bit away from the raucousness of the other girls.

'She's good at first and then she's not correcting his behaviour.'

'What could she do differently?'

'I could get onto it better,' Irene chimes in. All the girls are incredibly good at accepting the feedback. I've always been surprised by this, as the corporate people I work with are often far less open to 'owning it' than these kids are. Maybe they're used to receiving more criticism so it's just how life is for them, but either way, I find their honesty and openness about what they need to work on really refreshing.

Sam switches the video to another pairing and we watch Jana get her horse to stop with complete precision. 'How do you get him to do that?' one of the other girls asks.

'Everybody listens to me when I tell them what to do. That's just how I roll.' Looking at her, 45 kilograms of tough muscle, with faint marks on her forearms as evidence of self-harm, I can't help but wonder if fourteen-year-old Jana is as hard on herself as she is on everyone around her. It's true— the girls are just afraid enough of her to do what she says. She later tells Sam's mum, who's there looking after our daughter Tilly, that she's already left school. I don't know if it's true, but she says it in such a commanding way that no one questions her. No wonder she can keep her horse at a distance.

The video critique continues, with Sam leading the girls, encouraging them to learn appropriate language for offering constructive feedback, and giving each of them a chance to articulate for themselves what they could have done differently. I sometimes wonder who these kids would be if they had the kinds of lives that would allow them to pause and watch the video of what they had been doing, then have a chance to articulate what they might want to do differently next time. At least they get a little practice with us, and I can only hope they will take it back to their regular lives.

As we move on to watching the girls trying to lunge their horses for the first time, only Sian seems to have got the right balance of energy and clarity of communication to get her horse to run in a circle around her. While she doesn't say much, and she's told me she has no experience of horses, she seems to develop a bond with each of the horses she works with so they seem like two friends out playing together, like Bobby and I once were a long time ago. In one of the quieter moments I let her know she's a natural with horses, as she's probably never had that kind of feedback. She blushes and just looks at her horse, as if to say he's done everything and she was just along for the ride. I like that humility in her, as it's something no one can teach; it's just there or it isn't.

In one of the quieter moments I let her know she's a natural with horses, as she's probably never had that kind of feedback.

As the girls watch their lunging videos most of them realise, even before I say it, they've brought no energy to the situation. We did lunging at the end of the third session and Yella, the blonde Palomino we'd only just acquired, had put Sian through her paces, which is why it was so great to see her making the progress she did. Ngaio hadn't been there that week, but the other girls, Jana and Irene, had shown no energy in their lunging and the horses responded by giving them a lacklustre response. Considering how little they brought to the situation, I was surprised the horses hadn't fallen asleep on them.

'So, what are you going to do different this time?' I ask.

'More energy,' they chorus in unison, and then collapse into giggles. Sam asks each of the girls what they want to work on this week, and Sian, Jana and Irene all answer 'Energy'. Ngaio, who is obviously feeling a bit on the back foot, having missed the last session, says 'Communication' instead. I was glad they all felt as if they had a single concrete thing they could pay attention to during the session, and it gave me a touchpoint for asking them how they were doing with each of the tasks.

BEFORE THE GIRLS ARRIVED, I had gone down to the lower paddock where the horses were and created something of a confidence course for them. Striped poles lay on the ground at intervals—some singles, others in parallel with a horse-width space between them. I had put two big blue tarps down as well, knowing the horses wouldn't like the colour or the sound they made.

We had tied up four of the horses beforehand. There was Boo, the little white pony who could be as stubborn as a mule, but was just the right height to attract a lot of neck hugs and cuddles; Shaheen, Sam's four-year-old dappled-grey–Arab cross, whose face was slathered with sunscreen which would transfer itself to the girls' hands as they tried to pat his face; Yella, the new Palomino who was something of a mystery to us as we didn't know much about her past when it came to groundwork; and Chance, my twelve-year-old bay brood mare whom I've been training as my demonstration horse.

I take my time pairing the girls as I want to make sure they're getting new challenges each week. For this session, Jana and Yella become the two blondes, Jana's hair only slightly brassier than Yella's pale mane. Sian, who'd been so good with Yella the week before, goes off with Chance, who towers over her in height but follows her dutifully like a trained puppy. Irene, whose energy was all over the place last week, wants Cool Guy, but I want her to work with a horse who has more discipline. She and Cool Guy were both a bit gangly and met each other with the same degree of distract-edness. Instead, Irene and Shaheen are paired, and initially I can see she is out of her depth with him. Ngaio goes with Boo. Sam has pointed out to her that Boo has a puncture wound and she needs to be careful around it (it's hard to miss as the antibacterial spray around it is bright blue), and Ngaio frets for a good part of the morning over whether or not she is hurting her horse. She alternates between hugging him and dragging him by the lead around the paddock. Boo is always a lesson in patience.

I ask the girls to spend some time revisiting what they have done in the previous three sessions with their other horses in an attempt to build a new relationship with their horse of the day. They are all eager to get started, and within minutes they have spread out to different areas of the paddock. Most of them forget the other girls almost immediately as they become completely absorbed in what they are doing with their own horses.

Most of them forget the other girls almost immediately as they become completely absorbed in what they are doing with their own horses.

Jana looks fantastic getting Yella to stop and start, the horse following her pretty obediently around the paddock. Initially Jana's body language made her unapproachable, but as she works with Yella over the span of the morning she begins to hug him, and in the end she spends almost as much time rubbing him as she does working him. Whenever I go over to see how she is doing, she says, 'We're both blonde and stubborn. We totally get each other,' and I can see they do.

What I can see even more is how she and Sian, who have both lost their mothers, are becoming kids again in the company of their horses. As adults we often forget that kids who go through losing a parent young have to take on responsibility at an early age, whether they like it or not. What is beautiful—and it's something I've seen with other kids who've been through the same programme—is that the horses let them put aside being an adult for a while and just become kids again. It may be they are still in charge of the situation, which is why they are able to get their horses to do what they ask, but it's almost as if the horse invites them to relax and have fun.

I'm thinking about this as I watch Chance running

behind Sian, the girl's long ponytail blowing in the wind just like Chance's real tail. 'Stop!' she says quietly, but with such force that Chance skids to a stop in front of her. She leans in and puts her forehead to Chance's, then gives her a heart-to-heart 'Good girl!' I have the feeling that Chance, who is mother to Cool Guy, is saying the same thing back to her.

The horses let them put aside being an adult for a while and just become kids again.

Meanwhile, Irene has taken to heart the lesson about needing to keep her energy up if she wants to get Shaheen to lunge around her. To start with she was still giving him the same sort of sloppy slouching she had been doing before and Shaheen pretty much ignored her. Then, and I wish I knew exactly what it was that made her click, the next time I look over at her, she is standing tall while the big grey horse dances in a circle around her. All morning long Irene has been calling out to everyone, wanting attention, then suddenly she has become completely absorbed in what is happening around her and she goes quiet. It's like watching her go from child to adult in the span of a minute. She is now tall and commanding, and Shaheen circles her because she demands it through everything she is conveying to him.

As her arms begin to tire she slows him down to a stop and quietly pats his nose before yelling out, 'Ew!' as she remembers too late how much sticky suncream is on his nose. 'That's OK, boy. At least you won't get a sunburn,' she tells him.

She doesn't look around to see if the other girls have noticed how well she is doing, but Sam has been quietly filming her. I reflect that next week's video session will probably be completely different for her when she sees what an amazing change has taken place in the way she is holding herself and getting Shaheen to do what she asks.

This is the beauty of this course for me, and the leadership course, as you watch someone's transformation taking place right before your eyes. One moment there's slouchy Irene with not enough energy to inspire a horse to do anything but take an afternoon nap, then suddenly something clicks and she's got 600 kilograms of horse running in circles around her, and stopping when she wants him to stop. My sense is that because it's such physical work, the girls take the experience deep down in themselves. Even if they only get a few of these moments of success where they're in sync with their horse and get the results they want, it's more than they normally experience in their daily lives. So the memories of these moments are going to stand out for them all the more.

As I stand there Jana comes over to me and says, 'I don't want to switch horses anymore. For the rest of the course can it just be Yella and me?'

I have a think for a moment and realise something else has happened for the girls. They are forming relationships that matter to them. Now they want to commit to them. How can I say no?

I take a quick poll of the girls and, other than Ngaio, who has spent the better part of the morning struggling with Boo, the rest want to stay with their partners for the rest of the course. With that knowledge, they start to take on the confidence course. I notice each of them becomes more patient, and I wonder if it's because now they've made a commitment and there's going to be continuity in their relationship, so it's more important for them to see their horse succeed.

Sian is the first to get her horse across the blue tarp. She spends her time getting Chance to walk backwards through the parallel poles, frustrated but completely absorbed when Chance steps out of the poles and has to start again. She never loses her temper and doesn't ask for help. I like her quiet determination.

Irene, after her success in lunging, is determined that now Shaheen will be good at everything she does with him. He's not quite as interested as he was before so she walks him around the paddock for a while to change the scenery. In past classes she has required so much attention that I'm amazed at this new side of her. Now she is getting all the attention she needs from Shaheen, so I can watch from a distance.

Yella is giving Jana trouble for the first time that day. Sam goes over to see how she's doing and Jana tells her what she's told me, 'We're both just blonde and stubborn, that's all.'

Sam asks her what she does in her normal life when she notices she's being stubborn, and how she gets past it to solve things. 'I've never thought about it,' Jana replies seriously. 'Hmmm, I've really never thought about it.'

She turns to Yella, 'What do you think?' They go back to trying again.

The two hours disappear in a flash and soon Derek comes out to let the girls know it's time to head back. Sam takes photos of each girl with her horse, which she'll send on to them later to help remind them of the experience. I see them all holding onto their horses, whispering things to them, nose to nose.

'I don't want to go,' Jana says quietly. 'Yella might miss me when I go.'

'I'm sure she will,' I tell her, as she gives the horse one more hug. 'Don't worry, girl,' she says, 'I'll be back soon. We'll get it right next time, too.'

Up at the house Jana says in passing she can't go out with the other girls later because she has to do the grocery shopping for her father. 'He'd starve without me,' she says to no one in particular. I keep thinking about her with her arms draped around Yella's big neck, and how out in the paddock she was just a fourteen-year-old girl with her horse. Inside, texting on her phone with one hand and talking to her girlfriends at the same time, she has her life-armour back on for another week. I'm glad Yella let her put it away, even for a couple of hours.

As they're leaving, Derek leans over to me and says, 'Thanks for that. I saw a whole other side of those girls today I've never seen before. I wish I had the budget to bring every kid in the region to you. It was so cool to see the girls like that.'

While I'm sure he's seen sides of the girls that I'm glad

I never did, I keep thinking it's really not so much what I do,
but the gift the horses offer them, and everyone.

The chance just to be yourself.

How cool is that?

New beginnings

CHANCE

Eight years ago, when I was still working up the coast from Wellington, I received a phone call from an owner who was looking for someone to work some magic on a horse he had in training. She was beating her galloping partners with ease on the training track and had some real speed, but when it came to trials she had finished twenty lengths behind the last horse. No one could work out why she was underperforming, as there was no question she could really gallop.

When I saw her for the first time I thought, 'She's so skinny.' But that first glance showed me some of the reasons why she wasn't performing. She had a nice frame on her, but she had rainscald (lots of little scabs) all over her back, mudrash down her legs (more scabs stuck to her skin), a slightly runny nose, a wicked sunburn on that nose, and terrible feet. And she was thin and very weak.

Naturally, I was keen to get started with her to see if I could turn her around so she could be the winner I knew she really was. Into the hosing bay she went, with an all-over medicated wash over her back and down her legs. While she was drying, I gave her nose a good clean-out and put some Breatheasy in there, which is like Vicks for horses, to help her breathe better. My next job was to lightly wash the outside of her nose and put on some cream to soothe the sunburn, then put a spray on her back to help with the rain-scald. Then she was let into a yard with a biscuit of hay and a good feed.

She was a really nice, big, showy-looking horse if you could picture how she *could* look. Horses are like houses in a way. Just as some people are able to look at a rundown old cottage and imagine how it will look when it's been totally done up and freshly painted, I have always been able to look at a horse in any condition and picture what it will be like when it is healthy and well fed. This horse was tall, leggy and very athletic, all bay in colour except for a white stripe down her nose and three white socks. I could imagine she'd be a knockout when she was back to herself again.

I rang my vet and booked her in for a type of vitamin boost injection, along with an appointment with the horse dentist. I also called my farrier to make an appointment to have her feet cleaned up, then I got the massage therapist to come out and have a good look over her body. Apart from her obvious problems, I wanted to know if her teeth were sore (it turned out they were) and if that was the cause of her lack of condition. I also wanted to see if there was soreness in her body that was stopping her from trying (there was, so she had a couple of massages). I ordered an ulcer treatment for her, a paste that is given over a few days to clean the insides out. Stomach ulcers cause a burning of the stomach lining and can stop a horse performing.

I have always been able to look at a horse in any condition and picture what it will be like when it is healthy and well fed.

After I'd lined up all those treatments I gave her a drench, which is something I always do, and I think everyone should do when a horse comes on to a new property, to guard against worms and parasites. Then I put a cover and neck rug on her and led her out to a paddock. I chose one where she could be on her own, but with horses all around her for company. Horses, being very social animals, should always have a mate. It's the best way to make them happy. But because she had a slightly running nose and I wanted to really feed her up and give her some energy, for the present she had the paddock to herself.

I put four big bundles of beautiful red clover hay in her paddock and watched her have a run around and take in her new surroundings. It was paradise for a horse! Plenty of grass, post-and-rail fencing, horses everywhere, and a really happy environment. I started feeding her three times a day and gave her as much hay as she wanted. For the first two weeks I walked her fast in the morning for an hour, which I love doing with the horses as it builds stamina and strength and tones the body but doesn't take any weight off them. I wanted to get her looking stronger and more powerful. After her walk she would go out into the paddock, then mid-afternoon she would come in and I would run her through my system to build a relationship, work with her attitude, and release a lot of her tension and worry.

In the first couple of weeks we made huge progress. I wanted her to be able to participate in the jumpouts, which were coming up in three weeks' time, so as soon as her strength had improved a bit and she had put on some weight, I got back into some riding work. Her steering was horrible, so we did a lot of exercises in the arena to soften her up in the mouth and make her more supple, until she was beautiful and responsive.

We were building a special relationship now. She was such a big softy and just loved rubs and all the praise. She was really growing in confidence, had a spring back in her step, and was starting to fill out and look better every week. I took her up to Otaki and she had a couple of gallops in between some long walk and trot sessions at the beach. In the mornings I would call her, and wherever she was in the paddock she would look up, turn round and gallop up to me, then she'd put her head down to meet the head collar.

She was feeling really good in herself now. Her attitude was spot on and she was just so keen to please. She knew I was helping her, and she had put all her trust in me. In the last few days before the jumpouts I eased off her work—I wanted her on her toes and fresh, so we just did an hour's walk and lots of groundwork.

We were building a special relationship now. She was such a big softy and just loved rubs and all the praise.

Three weeks flew by and at last the day arrived, the chance to see if the last five weeks of hard work had been worth it. Her owner came up from Wellington. He was thrilled, and said she was looking a million dollars. I thought she was starting to look great, but being a perfectionist I could still picture a little more improvement. But after just five weeks there was no way she could have looked any better than she did.

I was feeling pretty confident. I knew she was fast and her mind was spot on. I had a chat to the jockey and told him that in the past two trials she had hung quite badly—when she went around a corner she went too wide and lost a lot of ground—so just to cover our bases he should keep her on the rail with a horse on her outside, to make it harder for her if she tried to do that.

We watched eagerly. The horses jumped out of the gates. She sprang out quickly and sat on the rail in third place in a field of eight. As they rounded the turn she moved out from the others, hit the front halfway down the straight, then pulled away to win by three lengths. Her owner and I were so excited we jumped around and did a quick high five in the stands, which is quite a bit of emotion for me as I'm usually very laidback. We were acting like we had won the Melbourne Cup, and when we glanced around, the others in the stand were looking at us as if to say, 'Settle down! It's just a jumpout. It doesn't mean anything.' But to us, knowing her history, it felt amazing.

In five weeks we had turned her around from coming in twenty lengths behind the last horse to winning by three lengths. Not a bad result for the first racehorse I had worked with.

In five weeks we had turned her around from coming in twenty lengths behind the last horse to winning by three lengths.

That horse was Chance, and now, eight years later, she is grazing down below the house, surrounded by the Remarkables and mountains on all sides. When I look at her now it's hard to imagine she could be any better. She has a new job, too. After two wins and six placings, she came back to me quite run down, so I decided to make her a brood mare instead. She produced a beautiful son, Cool Guy, who is now three. He will be my next venture into racing, after four years out, since Chance last raced. She has now been promoted from brood mare, to become my new demonstration horse.

But just when I thought she was mine, Sam has fallen in love with her because she looks so good and is moving like a superstar. Eventing could just be Chance's next chapter in the winner's circle. I can't wait to see what happens next.

IN MY YOUNGER YEARS, I would often be sitting down with a coffee in hand at seven o'clock in the evening, with two horses still to work. I would look at the slogan on the wall of the stables which reads: 'If it is to be, it is up to me'. I would go, tired as I was, to work those last horses, finishing around nine. I've never lost the belief that when someone is safe, has what he needs, and is leading a good life, just about anything is possible.

What I had never thought about until then was what life might feel like when all the sources of my happiness had started to slip away. Some of this was the result of overwork. I was burnt out and was losing the passion for my work, as life had become just one horse after another. Some was the result of what had happened in my relationship. But as I came into my late thirties I could see Rock mirroring back to me a guy who was just going through the motions. I knew I was tired and not myself. The horses could see it in me.

I knew I had to find a new direction, and I knew I had to believe in it. I was searching for my next step. Though my partner and I had split up, and we'd had some rough times, we still kept our business going as we had finally built it to a good place. I was proud of the work we were doing in helping both young people and adults to gain more confidence and knowledge through their experiences with the horses.

My reputation had been growing over the years, and now I started doing again what I had done earlier, running courses all around the country, teaching people how to read, understand and get the best from their horses, along with specific problem-solving. Thinking back on how much I had enjoyed the time I had spent at Mt Nicholas Station, I ran a two-week breaking-in course at the beautiful Closeburn Station in Queenstown, teaching owners how to start their young horses. Then out of the blue I received a phone call from the owner of a five-star resort in Tonga: would I consider coming over for ten days and helping them with a couple of horses for a few hours each day. This was something I couldn't turn down, and it was an amazing experience. So there were glimmers of hope on the horizon, but nothing sustaining. And there was a lot of grief; it was during this time that King Guru came and went from my life.

And it was also at this time that I met a woman named Cindy, who had a beautiful property in Dalefield, the valley between Queenstown and Arrowtown. Not long before, she had lost her husband when a tree fell on his vehicle as he was driving down the road. As she was figuring out her life again, her home became something like a place of healing for a number of us who were also grieving. I used to stay with her when I came down to Queenstown, and she had a way of making me feel good about myself again. I'd come in from a day's work in the area and she'd be making dinner and would just want to hear about my day—who I'd met, what had been happening with the horses. Cindy is truly a wise woman, and she has become a great friend. Sometimes it's the person who listens to you and has time for you who makes all the difference in the world.

Sometimes it's the person who listens to you and has time for you who makes all the difference in the world.

Because Cindy was also involved with horses, I met a lot of people in the community through her. I loved that part of the country, so I started running more courses down there. A beautiful woman named Sam came to one of my early courses, and I couldn't help but notice her. After the first course she asked me to keep in touch, and while my life was a little complicated at the time, I kept the thought in the back of my mind.

Sam had split up from her husband not long before and she, too, had found solace at Cindy's kitchen table. Cindy let her graze her horse on the property and Sam was often there, but usually I'd only see her race in, then race out again. She would only have a small window of time when she could go for a ride while her mother looked after her two daughters.

One night I asked Sam out to the Blue Door, a little bar in Arrowtown, just as friends. As we sat by the fire and talked, it turned out that everything we wanted in life was similar. She loved horses, had been involved with them her whole life, and we cared about so many of the same things. It just felt easy and right.

I still had some things to untangle in my life, but with Sam, I felt hopeful again. In time, I moved down to Queenstown and we found a property to rent where we could keep our horses and run our courses. Sam shared my dreams, and we began again with a new business, one of our own. I see Luca every other week, and he and Sam's daughters adore each other.

And speaking of daughters, our own daughter, Matilda, or Tilly, as we call her, came into the world in May 2015. If you'd told me in the depths of the dark times I'd have a daughter in a few years who could brighten my heart the way she does, I never would have believed it. But it's amazing what can happen and how good the world can turn out to be.

Rock moved down to Dalefield along with Chance and Cool Guy. They met Sam's horse, Shaheen, and together we've brought new horses like Yella into our fold. Sam's very good at finding horses for sale that she'd love to bring home. I can remember the days of having 25 horses on the go all the time, so sometimes I have to caution her a little, and remind her that maybe we should just enjoy the ones we already have. She usually agrees.

Tilly has just turned one and is already walking everywhere. She's all go, that little girl. I can't wait until she can learn to ride. Already the horses seem to smile every time she comes out to the paddock with me. While I didn't grow up on the back of a horse, I get the feeling she just might. And I can only begin to imagine the places she'll go.